The Chorale

the Chorale

*Through Four Hundred Years of
Musical Development as a
Congregational Hymn*

by Edwin Liemohn

Muhlenberg Press   Philadelphia

Printed in U. S. A.

UB732

Preface

The study of the chorale and church music in general has been a subject of vital concern to a number of European writers over a considerable period. At times this type of research has become an end in itself and has contributed little toward the general improvement of the chorale and congregational singing.

This volume sets forth the salient factors in the history of the chorale in the Scandinavian countries and Germany. By using two of Luther's melodies: *Ein feste Burg ist unser Gott* and *Vom Himmel hoch,* an attempt has been made to show how these melodies have been treated from the time of their first appearance up into the twentieth century. The reader is cautioned to keep in mind that throughout the first part of this period extensive changes were taking place in music as it developed toward the type of expression which makes possible the chorale form as known today.

Since only fragmentary material on the chorale is to be found in the English language, except for a small volume treating only the origin and influence of the earliest chorale melodies, a considerable portion of the material presented here is based on the research of Danish, Norwegian, Swedish, and German writers. I therefore solicit suggestions on areas which appear to have been slighted and ask that any errors be called to my attention. That this volume may be of help in understanding some problems of our church music today is the hope of its author.

Wartburg College   EDWIN LIEMOHN
Waverly, Iowa
January 1, 1953

Acknowledgments

In addition to the great many who assisted so graciously in procuring the materials necessary for this study, I owe a special debt of gratitude to two of my colleagues, Professors Erna Moehl and Walter Tillmanns, who rendered invaluable assistance in the final preparation of the manuscript. Not least do I value the forbearance and personal sacrifices of Clara which made it possible for me to undertake this study.

E. L.

Contents

CONTENTS

Monodic and Polyphonic Techniques
1524-1586

THE STATE OF MUSIC IN THE EARLY
SIXTEENTH CENTURY

European music was in its early stages of development at the time of the Reformation. While the present system of notation had its beginnings in the tenth century—with the use of the four-line staff becoming quite common by the middle of the eleventh century—an approximation of the present system of notation came with the adoption of the five-line staff —first used only for vocal music—in the fifteenth century. In Germany, however, the older neumatic notation, written without a staff, continued in use as late as the fourteenth century. The systematic use of more modern devices, such as bar lines, was not universal until the eighteenth century although some composers had used bar lines in the modern manner a half century earlier. Bar lines as used in the sixteenth century—the period of the Reformation—merely indicated breathing places in singing and did not indicate the end of a measure.

The concept of modern major and minor tonality was just emerging on the musical horizon in the early sixteenth century. The old ecclesiastical modes were still used although, with the freer use of chromaticism and the extensive interest in opera beginning in Italy at the close of the sixteenth century, the old modal system was breaking down. The transition from modal to tonal music (i.e., to major and minor scale structures) was very gradual and progressed as an understanding of basic harmonic laws increased. The great Flemish composer, Josquin des Prés (d. 1521) used harmonic devices experimentally but quite successfully. It was not until the seventeenth century, however, that composers and theoreticians understood harmony to the point where it could be effectively employed on a broad basis.

The English composer, William Byrd (d. 1623) and the Italians, Carissimi (d. 1674) and Monteverdi (d. 1643) stand out as composers whose command of the modern major and minor tonalities ended the popular use of the modal system. Composition in the first century of the Reformation period is therefore seen to lie mostly within the domain of traditional modal music.

Part music had its first great period of development in the Netherland school of the fifteenth and early sixteenth centuries. This group of composers demonstrated a fine command of what was essentially a polyphonic technique, based on the association of two or more voices singing independent parts simultaneously, generally employing imitation. Each part was melodic and complete in itself, and a pleasing combination resulted when each was combined with one or more additional voices.

The following examples will serve as illustrations of this type of music.

PLENI SUNT COELI[1]

Josquin des Prés

Ple - - - - - - - - - -

Ple -

-   *etc.*

- - - - - - - - *ni* - - - - - - - - - - - - - - - - - - - *sunt* - - - - - - - - - - -

ZWISCHEN BERG UND TIEFEM TAL[2]

Heinrich Isaac

Zwi-schen Berg und tie - - - fem Tal, zwi - schen

Zwi - schen   Berg   und   tie - - -

Zwi - schen

---

[1] From the Mass *Pange Lingua.* Copyright by Mercury Music Corporation, New York. Reprinted by permission.

[2] 111, No. 87. Used with the permission of the publisher, the Harvard University Press. Number references refer to books listed in the Bibliography.

3

The independence of melodic movement and the use of imitation are both very apparent in these two illustrations. These excerpts are illustrations of the highest type of music produced at the beginning of the sixteenth century which is the period of the Reformation. A basic characteristic of the use of imitation has remained in popular use in the modern "round."

While both of these illustrations are distinctly of the polyphonic and imitation type, some music of the period, particularly in the works of Josquin des Prés, makes use of full chords with the voices moving together in a uniform rhythmic pattern. However necessary as it was for the complete development of the chorale, the science of harmony, even in its rudimentary forms, was not well understood until the end of the sixteenth century.

Another factor of tremendous importance in this period was the invention of printing. While the printing press had been invented in the fifteenth century and music had been printed as early as 1476, it was not until the following century that the art of printing music was mastered to a workable degree. The invention of printing together with the beginnings of harmony at the close of the sixteenth century brought the art of music into a period of unprecedented growth. In this development, the chorale played an important role.

EARLY REFORMATION MUSIC IN GERMANY

The adaptation and influence of the chorale

The term *chorale* (or *choral*) did not originate with the Reformation movement. It had been used to designate the early plain song of the Roman office, sometimes spoken of as the Gregorian choral, or Gregorian chant. This included such numbers as the Kyrie, Gloria in Excelsis, Credo, Sanctus, Benedictus, Agnus Dei, and also the Introits, Offertories, and Tracts. The term was later applied specifically to designate the congregational hymn of the evangelical church. In the second half of the sixteenth century music developed a feeling for melodic symmetry and rhythm in a type of music consisting of melody with a supporting harmony. The church hymn aided in this development with its regular poetical construction resulting in singing each line of verse to a separate melodic phrase, usually one note to each syllable or monosyllabic word.

The influence of the chorale on the development of music is recognized not only by church musicians but by musicologists of all periods in the development of the art. In the words of a contemporary historian:

The musical tradition to which it gave extraordinary impetus not only during the sixteenth but in later centuries was to be a fundamental part of German music. . . . The language of religion was to be the language of the congregation and the musical part of the service was to be entered into by the worshippers. These two aims were the direct cause of a new musical tradition, the modifying influence of which was a powerful factor in shaping the development of music in England and northern Germany. . . . the musical aspect of the work of Martin Luther and his followers had, for the future, an influence similar to that which would have been exerted by a strong and revolutionary school of composition.[3]

_____
[3] 11, pp. 166, 177.

5

Commenting on the influence these early melodies played in the development of music, Wilson states that from 1524 to 1750 (the death of J. S. Bach), "The chorale melodies run like golden threads through nearly all the finest work of German composers."[4] A great deal of the music produced by German composers in this period is based on the chorale.

The hymn of the Reformation was destined to be one of the greatest single factors to make a lasting contribution to the development of music as an art. The transformation of the old chorale of the Roman church into its present manner of dress, however, was not to be completed until in the nineteenth century. Its development as a musical composition continued hand in hand with the development of music as an art.

Luther's problem and solution

The problem for Luther was to restore to the common people the vernacular congregational hymn which had for the most part been removed by the Roman church. He was certain that music should have an important role in the church service and also that the congregation should take part. As early as the fourth century the Council of Laodicea had ruled that "Beside the Psalmsingers appointed thereto, who mount the Ambo and sing out of the Book, no others shall sing in church." The musical part of the service was therefore taken over by the clergy and the choir while congregational hymn singing fell into disuse. This action by the church was prompted at least in part by the fact that hymn writing and hymn singing had fallen into disrepute because of the extensive use of hymns by heretical groups such as the Arians and Gnostics. Congregational singing was therefore permitted only for special occasions or

[4] 38, p. 6.

for minor services and for the production of religious plays.

The restoration of popular congregational hymn singing was a matter of vital concern to the evangelical church during the first century of its existence. Early Reformation forces, however, found comparatively few vernacular hymns in use. Schweitzer states that some German hymns had gained admission into the religious service of the Roman church "under cover of the *Kyrie* and *Alleluia.*"[5] These were songs of a liturgical character which ended with the refrain *Kyrieeleis* or *Alleluia,* and were permitted on very special occasions to be sung by the congregation. Verses in German were inserted among the lines of the liturgy also as a means of interpreting the Latin text.

The need of expressing their devotional feelings in their own language was urgent with the Germans and this need had to be satisfied. Luther insisted that the hymns be in the language of the people. Many of the new German hymns in use in the early period of the Reformation came from his pen. In a letter to Nicolaus Hausmann, pastor at Zwickau, Luther wrote:[6]

I explained to this publisher the manner in which to sing German: this I would like very much to have introduced here.

On another occasion he wrote:

I also wish as many of the songs as possible to be in the vernacular, which the people should sing during Mass either immediately after the *Gradual,* and immediately after the *Sanctus* and *Agnus Dei.* For who doubts that once upon a time all the people sang these, and now only the choir sings or responds when the bishop is consecrating? . . . they may be sung either right after the Latin songs, or on alternate days, now Latin, now the vernacular, until the entire Mass shall be made vernacular.[7]

---

[5] 118, Vol. I, p. 5.
[6] 121, Vol. VI, p. 137.
[7] 121, Vol. VI, p. 98.

In solving the problem of supplying vernacular hymns for the new faith, Luther found at his disposal the following main resources:

1. The official Latin hymnody, which included plain song melodies, melodies from Latin sequences, and from later popular Latin hymns written by monks. From this source he took both the music and the texts which were then translated.

2. The pre-Reformation popular hymns. These were actually religious folk songs which had collected over centuries. From these he used the texts, melodies, or both.

3. Secular song melodies, sometimes with parts of the original secular texts. These were either secular folk songs, or melodies by contemporary composers sung to secular texts.

4. Melodies written especially for the Lutheran service.

The following examples will serve as illustrations from the above sources.

1. A plain song melody:[8]

VENI CREATOR SPIRITUS

This hymn had been translated into German by the twelfth century. Hymns of this type needed little revision in the text but melodies often had to be altered considerably. It appeared

---

[8] 83, p. 46.

as follows in the *Erfurter Enchiridion* of 1525:[9]

KOMM GOTT SCHOPFER, HEILIGEN GEIST

Ten years later, in Klug's *Gesangbuch,* it appeared in the following version which is almost identical with present-day versions of the melody:[10]

2. The following is a pre-Reformation hymn taken over by

---

[9] 122, No. 294.

[10] 122, No. 295. It is interesting to note that the 1940 Episcopal hymnal has this notation of the melody (No. 108):

which has more decorative turns than the *Erfurter Enchiridion* version.

the Reformation. From this source, often both the original words and melody were used.[11]

NUN BITTEN WIR DEN HEILIGEN GEIST

The Gregorian melodies and the pre-Reformation, sacred, folk song melodies were altered to the extent necessary to make them conform more closely to the rhythmic structure of secular folk melodies. The secular folk melodies in themselves constituted the greatest single store of melodies for church use.

The following example of a secular song pressed into service by the evangelical church shows both the original text and the hymn version derived from it.

3. A secular song:[12]

O WELT ICH MUSS DICH LASSEN

---

[11] As given in Walther's *Gesangbüchlein* of 1524. From 38, p. 61.
[12] 38, p. 61.

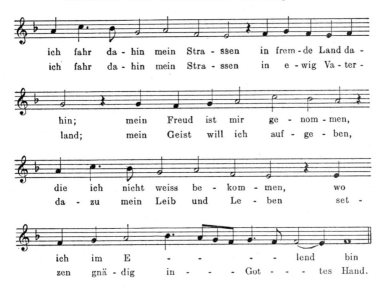

ich fahr da - hin mein Stra - ssen in frem - de Land da -
ich fahr da - hin mein Stra - ssen in e - wig Va - ter -

hin; mein Freud ist mir ge - nom - men,
land; mein Geist will ich auf - ge - ben,

die ich nicht weiss be - kom - men, wo
da - zu mein Leib und Le - ben set -

ich im E - - - - lend bin
zen gnä - dig in - - - Got - - - tes Hand.

The secular version of this number is first found about 1475, and it came into sacred use about 1505. It appeared in the Nuremberg hymnbook of 1569. The melody was given a four-part setting by Heinrich Isaac in the latter part of the fifteenth century. While the melody is of doubtful origin, it is generally considered to be of secular origin, either as a folk tune, or written by Isaac.

4. From the fourth source of chorale melodies—those composed specially for the new faith—a great number are found in currently used hymnals. The first half of the sixteenth century produced comparatively few original melodies, with Johann Walther and Martin Luther being the most prominent composers of hymn melodies. For the many hymnals with their hundreds of hymns published between 1524 and 1545, a total of only about two hundred melodies were available.

The use of secular melodies

Why should it be necessary for the early evangelical church to pirate secular songs and adapt them for its use? There appear to be three reasons. First, there was a dire need for melodies. The number of melodies never kept pace with the number of hymn texts. Secondly, there was little difference between the features of a melody originally associated with a secular text and one written particularly for a sacred text. The reason for this is found in the fact that throughout the Middle Ages the practice of music was essentially within the church. Those who taught and those who studied were associated with the work of the church and many melodies written for secular texts were produced by the same men who wrote melodies for church use. These men had been trained in one technique in musical composition: the technique which produced music suitable for church use. Often the full beauty of these melodies was not brought out until they were associated with a sacred text. Even some of the secular melodies of the minnesingers and Meistersingers made quite acceptable hymn tunes. Hans Sachs, the cobbler who belonged to the latter group, made several notable contributions, including a hymn honoring the Reformation.[13] Hans Sachs is only one of a group of people who supplied the wherewithal needed in the evangelical service. Bakers, bootmakers, tailors, and other tradesmen made their contributions. A hymnal prepared by Wizel in 1546 states that "... throughout half of Germany there is scarcely a pastor or a shoemaker who lacks the skill to make a little song or two to sing at church with his neighbors."[14]

---

[13] "Awake My Heart's Beloved, Thou Christian Church Most Dear." Pub. by H. W. Gray Co.

[14] 38, p. 3.

A third reason for the use of secular melodies is akin to the second. At the time of the Reformation there existed both religious and secular folk songs. There was a close bond between the two. Since the religious folk songs were appropriated by the church, why not modify the secular songs and use them too? They all came from a common culture. This reasoning no doubt seemed very sound. The two texts of *O Welt ich muss dich lassen* provide a good illustration of how this was done. Another example is found in *Er ist der Morgensterne* which became *O Christe Morgensterne,* and still another in *Aus fremden Landen komm' ich her* which became *Vom Himmel hoch da komm' ich her,* a popular Christmas hymn.

It is true that secular melodies were not always found to be satisfactory. This was the case particularly with melodies still in popular use and associated with texts which were far removed from religious thoughts. Luther found it necessary to discard the melody to which his *Vom Himmel hoch da komm' ich her* was first sung because it was still used in taverns and dance halls. A number of such melodies had to be discarded as unfit. For the above hymn, Luther is supposed to have written his own melody to which it is still sung. It appeared in a Leipzig hymnbook as early as 1539.

A basic working principle of the Reformation was to reshape the material at hand. For example, the translated title of a volume appearing in 1571 reads: *Street Songs, Cavalier Songs, Mountain Songs, Transformed into Christian and Moral Songs, for the abolishing in course of time of the bad and vexatious practice of singing idle and shameful songs in the streets, in fields, and at home, by substituting for them good, sacred, honest words.*[15]

---

[15] 118, Vol. I, p. 17.

The practice of converting secular melodies into chorale melodies has continued to some extent into our own time. An early seventeenth century illustration of this is Hassler's melody to which we sing *O Sacred Head, Now Wounded,* known as the *Passion Chorale.* Hassler wrote this melody in 1601 for a love song, the first line of which is: *Mein Gmüth ist mir verwirret, das macht ein Jungkfrau Zart.* Still no one will deny that this is a most acceptable hymn tune.

Referring to the use of secular melodies as chorale melodies, the German historian and theologian Köstlin remarks:

Who thinks when he hears the melodies *Nun ruhen alle Wälder* and *Herzlich thut mich verlangen* that the one originally belonged to the song of the itinerant artisans, *Insbruch ich muss dich lassen;* and that the other was composed by Hassler for a love-song? Who, when he sings the rather sombre *Kommt her zu mir spricht Gottes Sohn,* is reminded of the fact that the melody is no other than the old *Lindenschmittston,* which, set to countless songs, was widely popular in South Germany, and sung everywhere—in the street, in the spinning-room, and at the drinking-bout?[16]

Secular melodies were also appropriated from other countries. Referring to the use of such melodies, Schweitzer states "Any foreign melody that had charm and beauty was stopped at the frontier and pressed into the service of the evangelical service."[17] The melody for *Wenn wir in höchsten Nöten sind* was taken from the Huguenot Psalter, which in turn likely had appropriated it from secular folk song sources.

Chorale melodies have always been closely identified with folk music. The Gregorian chorales which are at the very basis of Western church music, are actually religious folk melodies. These chorales together with the religious folk melodies and

---

[16] 38, p. 41.
[17] 118, Vol. I, p. 19.

the secular folk melodies have all sprung from a common source.

Luther's contribution

After leaving the Wartburg, to which he had retired following the Diet of Worms in 1522, Luther began to plan his reforms in the church service. These were to include hymn singing as a regular feature of the service. His *Formula Missae,* a revision of the Latin Mass, published in 1523 touched on the matter of vernacular hymns stating "I wish that we had many German hymns which the people might sing in the Mass with the *Gradual,* the *Sanctus* and *Agnus Dei.*"[18]

In his *Deutsche Messe* (German Mass) of 1524, a German hymn displaced the Latin Introit at the beginning of the service. After the Epistle the hymn *Nun bitten wir den heiligen Geist* was introduced. After the Gospel the versified version of the Creed, *Wir glauben all' an einem Gott* was sung. At the administration of the Lord's Supper the German Sanctus, *Jesaia dem Propheten das geschah* or *Gott sei gelobet und gebenedeiet* or Huss's *Jesus Christus unser Heiland* would be sung, followed by the German Agnus Dei, *Christe du Lamm Gottes.*

Luther's great contribution was in writing hymns, supervising the preparation of hymnals, and in selecting appropriate melodies. He was not, and did not pretend to be, a great composer of music. While he was a musician of great understanding and some achievement, Johann Walther, cantor at the palace of Frederick the Wise at Torgau, and his associate in the cause of music for the Reformation—Conrad Rupff—were better qualified musically than Luther. Quoting again from Köstlin, a fancied description of how Luther may have assisted Walther and

---

[18] 38, pp. 19, 20.

Rupff in composing hymn tunes is given in these words:

While Rupff and Walther sat at the table bending over their music sheets, pen in hand, father Luther paced up and down, trying over on his fife the melodic phrases, which streamed from his memory and imagination to join themselves to the words of the hymn, until at length the tune was firmly established.[19]

Luther was well acquainted with the polyphonic technique of his day. On his journey to Rome in 1511 he became particularly interested in the music of Josquin des Prés and Ludwig Senfl, a pupil of Heinrich Isaac. The music of des Prés made a great impression on Luther, and this outstanding musician became Luther's favorite composer.

Trained as a monk, Luther had been well schooled in the musical part of the Roman service. This was the technique he had learned and this was the style which was to influence him in his own attempts at musical composition. Some critics take the extreme position that he wrote no melodies, while writers of about 1600 credit him with over 100 melodies. No doubt the overemphasis given his position as a composer in this period has enshrouded him in both a mystical and mythical veil which has since left historians very dubious in regard to his musical accomplishments. Nineteenth century research does not arrive at agreement, with Koch crediting him with eight melodies, Winterfeld with three, and others none. Early twentieth century research on the other hand is more generous. Moser is quite certain Luther wrote at least twenty melodies. Drawing his conclusions from the writings of Paul Eber (a Wittenberg pastor and hymn writer), Johann Walther (the outstanding musician of the early Reformation period and co-worker with Luther), the poet Spangenberg, and Sleidanus who wrote a history of

---

[19] 38, p. 8.

the Reformation in 1555, Moser states—in referring to fifty songs listed in the Weimar edition of Luther's works:

Therefore we can come to only one conclusion: that these four eye and ear witnesses have spoken the truth and that Luther at least is responsible for being the composer of the main body of the twenty Wittenberg melodies and that he is revisor of the twenty old churchly melodies. . .[20]

There is no serious question about his authorship of at least three melodies, those for the hymns *Ein feste Burg ist unser Gott, Vom Himmel hoch, da komm' ich her,* and *Jesaia dem Propheten das geschah.* Franz Horn in his booklet on the first of these three, *Ein feste Burg,* reproduces a copy of the melody which is supposed to be in Luther's handwriting. A copy of the melody as given there follows.[21]

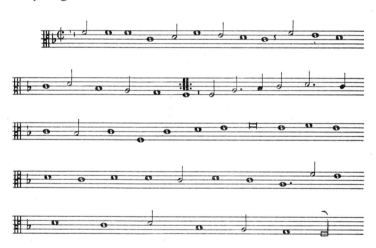

This was written in the C clef which was used at that time. In our modern G clef the melody assumes this appearance:

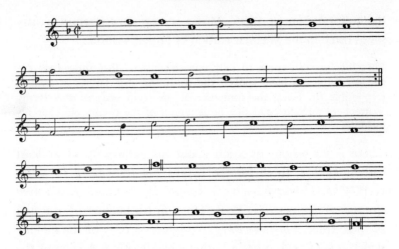

Other historians contend that this melody is taken from Gregorian chants. It is not altogether surprising that there should be a close similarity between Gregorian chants and any melody which Luther may have written. He could not very well have expressed himself in a style totally different from that in which he had received his musical training.

There is also evidence to show that Luther had some skill in counterpoint. Moser lists among his accomplishments a four-voice composition at the close of a Latin school drama *Lazarus redivivus,* adding a third part to a response after meals sung by his sons Martin and Paul, and adding a fourth voice to a three-voice composition to "put the musical smarty Rörer in Wittenberg in his place," as Luther wrote in a letter to a friend.[22]

Not only did Luther have an understanding and an appreciation of music, but he also believed it played an important part in everyday life. As given in the following quotation his attitude toward nonmusical people is not altogether charitable:

---

[22] 25, p. 20.

If any man despises music, as all fanatics do, for him I have no liking; for music is a gift and grace of God, not an invention of men. Thus it expels the Devil and makes men cheerful. Then one forgets all wrath, impurity, sycophancy, and other vices. Next to theology, I give music the highest and most honorable place. . ."[23]

In the training of pastors, Luther was also adamant when he expressed the opinion that young men should not be ordained as preachers unless they had been well trained in music.

Music in the early evangelical service

For about a century after the beginning of the Reformation movement, many Lutheran churches continued performing masses in Latin as well as in German. They performed not only masses of Catholic composers, but also some written in Latin by Lutheran composers. It was not until the close of the sixteenth century that the music of the evangelical church began to sever its relationship with Catholic music and assume individuality.

While Luther reinstated congregational singing as a regular feature of the church service, a chasm between Catholic and Lutheran music did not exist. The latter grew out of the former over a period of many years. The Gregorian chants which became hymn melodies continued in use. The choir continued singing music written for the Roman service, although some of the parts were now sung by the congregation in the German language.

"Where a choir existed," says Schweitzer, "the congregation took little part in the singing, being restricted to the *Credo* . . . and perhaps a communion hymn."[24] In the churches where no choir was available, more importance was attached to the congregational singing, with the Kyrie, Gloria, and Agnus Dei being sung in their German translations as hymns.

---

[23] 31, pp. 13, 14.
[24] 118, Vol. I, p. 31.

Continuing the parochial schools under their own leadership, the reformers were in a position to teach their hymns and the elements of music to the youth of the congregations. These schools had their music instruction under a cantor who in addition to teaching music was usually encumbered with sundry other tasks, such as lecturing on philosophy, teaching Hebrew, history, or possibly even mathematics. Here the cantor trained the choirs which would sing in church on Sundays. This pattern of school, cantor, choir, and church was to exist up through the time of J. S. Bach in the middle of the eighteenth century.

The parochial schools played a significant role in the development of Lutheran church music. Here the boys were put through a carefully graded study of music, starting with the simple chants and culminating in singing four- and eight-part compositions. The cantors usually lived with their pupils, trained them in their choir music and led them in their church performances.

Luther did not consider music as an independent art in its relation to the church but rather as a means of promoting the work of the church. His concept of music in the church was therefore somewhat akin to that of Pope Gregory the Great in the sixth century who realized the importance of music in the church although he had little interest in it as an art. Luther's purpose was to make music serve the common man, but in following such a program he did not preclude the possibility of its independent artistic development in the hands of serious composers for choir. In contrast to other Protestant leaders, Luther continued the services of the choir which sang the polyphonic church music of that period. In the field of music, as in his religious tenets, Luther's purpose was not to eradicate the musical part of the service but to reshape it to fit his scheme. While in the use of organs and polyphonic vocal music other reformers saw only undesirable appendages of the papacy, Luther saw in music a medium for enriching the service and in the congregational hymn a further means of spreading the doctrines of the new faith.

Early German publications

During his lifetime, Luther was privileged to see his *Ein feste Burg* given five musical settings by other composers, as follows:[25]

(a) For three voices with the melody in the tenor, in *Newe Gesang,* edited by Joannem Kugelmann, Augsburg, 1540.

(b) For four voices, with the melody in the bass, in *Newe deutsche geistliche Gesenge,* by G. Rhaw, Wittenberg, 1544.

(c) For five voices, melody in the tenor, by Stephen Mahu, in Rhaw's hymnbook.

(d) For four voices, melody in the bass, by M. Agricola, in Rhaw's hymnbook.

(e) For four voices, melody in the bass, by L. Hellinck, also in Rhaw's hymnbook.

Luther's melody appeared for the first time in a hymnal publication in 1529.

As seen in the above, the musical settings were for three, four, or five voices, with the melody either in the tenor or in the bass. The general practice in composition at that time was to have the melody in the tenor. These settings were for the choir only, and did not invite congregational participation. The following excerpt is the beginning of the setting by Stephen Mahu as it appeared in Rhaw's *Newe deutsche geistliche Gesenge.*[26]

---

[25] 113, Vol. III, p. 256.
[26] 94, No. 12 in issue No. 218.

This setting for five voices by Stephen Mahu has the melody in the tenor.

The music in the early period of the Reformation was therefore of two types: *monodic,* being the congregational hymn, sung in unison, and *polyphonic,* a more elaborate setting for choir. The position of the choir in the evangelical service was not appreciably altered as compared with its function in the Roman church. On the other hand, congregational singing in this period was not quite as important a factor as we are sometimes led to believe. The change-over from singing by a professional choir as was done in the Roman service to congregational singing as known today was not effected in a short time. Even so, the Lutheran church was far ahead of other Reformed church bodies who for the most part participated only in psalm singing and tolerated no choir nor organ.

In the preparation of hymnals for the use of the congregation, Luther had the precedent and encouragement of the successful use of a popular hymnody in the Hussite revival in Bohemia. The Hussites' first hymnal had been published in Prague in 1501, a collection of eighty-nine hymns for the church of the Bohemian Brethren. Michael Weisse, leader of a German group in Bohemia, brought out a hymnal in German for their use in 1531. This publication had 157 hymns and 112 melodies. Some of these were later incorporated into the Lutheran hymnals.

Since there were two types of musical settings employed by the Lutherans, there were also two types of hymn publications: the full musical setting of several voices for choir, and the small enchiridions—text editions usually with melodies—used by the congregation and for devotions in the home. Indications are that the enchiridions were intended primarily for home use and that the hymns contained therein should be sung in church after they had been learned in using them at home. It was Luther's wish that in the parochial schools the new hymns should first be taught to the children, who should then lead the congregation so that the older people would learn to sing the hymns more readily.

The first two small hymnals of the evangelical church were published in 1524. One was the *Etlich Christlich Lieder,* generally known as the *Achtliederbuch* since it contained only eight hymns, four of which were by Luther. The other of these earliest of Protestant hymnals was the *Erfurter Enchiridion* which contained twenty-six hymns.[27]

The Danish historian, O. E. Thuner, reproduces a page of the *Achtliederbuch* containing the following widely used hymn:[28]

---

[27] Some sources say twenty-five hymns.
[28] 120, p. 25.

NUN FREWDE EUCH LIEBEN CHRISTENN GEMAYN

The first great musical publication of the Reformation was Johann Walther's *Gesangbüchlein,* a collection of thirty-two hymns in polyphonic settings for choir. This collection was intended for the choirs trained in the parochial schools which sang at the Sunday services. For this book Luther wrote the first of his four hymnbook prefaces, which reads in part:

And these are arranged in four parts for no other reason than that I greatly desire the youth, who certainly should and must be trained in music and other proper and useful arts, to have something whereby they may be weaned away and freed from the love ballads and worldly (carnal) songs. . .[29]

Which of these three publications was issued first is not known. The *Achtliederbuch* probably carries the distinction of being the first since it appears unlikely that the *Erfurter Enchiridion,* a larger book, would precede the smaller. It appears also that the latter was published after Walther's *Gesangbüchlein* since its melodies were taken largely from Walther's book.

An important event in the publication of materials for the Reformation was the opening of a printing establishment in 1525 by George Rhaw (also spelled *Rhau*), a former cantor at the St. Thomas School and a lecturer in the university, both in

---

[29] 121, Vol. VI, p. 284.

Leipzig. He joined hands with the Lutheran movement, making his print shop a channel through which great quantities of materials, including hymnals and music publications became available.

The *Erfurter Enchiridion* became the basic hymnal for the early period of the Reformation. Several editions followed in rapid succession and a number of new hymnals were prepared based upon it. The editors of hymnals which appeared without Luther's authorization often took the liberty of altering the hymns to suit their own liking. Since it was a common practice to pirate publications, it soon became necessary for Luther to have a new hymnal prepared which would restore his hymns to their original version. This resulted in the *Geistliche Lieder auff new gebessert* (Spiritual Songs Recently Improved) which was published probably in 1529. In his preface to this book, Luther admonished:

. . . I realize that this daily, indiscriminate revising and supplementing, according to each individual's fancy, will reach no other end than that the longer our first hymns are printed the more false they will be in comparison with the originals. I fear the same thing will happen ultimately to this little book as has been the fate of good books in all times, namely that it will be completely submerged by the additions of bungling heads and make a desolate thing so that the good in it will be lost and only the good-for-nothing will be kept in use.[30]

No copy is known to exist of the original edition of this hymnal. The first reprint came out the same year as Klug's *Gesangbuch.* This, together with Klug's of 1535 and 1543, Schumann's of 1539, and Babst's of 1545, are for the most part reprints of Luther's *Geistliche Lieder* of 1529. Klug's of 1529 was the first to contain Luther's *Ein feste Burg* and his *Jesaia dem Propheten.*

---

[30] 121, Vol. VI, pp. 285-6.

Babst's hymnal of 1545 was the last brought out under Luther's direction. It contained 120 hymns and 97 melodies. This hymnal was subsequently reissued several times and remained the authoritative hymnal in use till about 1600.

Walther's *Gesangbüchlein* for choir also enjoyed popular use. By 1551 it had passed through five editions. An example of Walther's musical setting in this publication follows:[31]

ERBARM DICH MEIN, O HERRE GOTT

---

[31] 94, No. 71. Melody is in the tenor. Taken from the 1524 edition.

Even though over two hundred hymnbooks appeared between 1525-1575, the first half of the sixteenth century saw only a few specially composed hymn tunes, with Walther supplying more than any other. In his preface to a hymnal of German and Latin funeral hymns published in 1542, Luther states that:

... we have chosen fine musical settings or songs which are used in the papacy at vigils. . .[32]

This may be an indication that a shortage of good hymn tunes still persisted although Luther was not opposed to using good tunes originally associated with Latin texts. The practice of including Latin songs in Protestant hymnals continued for some time. A hymnal published in 1551 contained a total of 125 hymns of which 47 were in Latin.

This dual-language problem had its difficulties even in the pre-Reformation period. While the scholarly minded leaders accepted a thorough knowledge of Latin as a part of their training, the common people showed little interest in the language. Because of their insistence that some of the vernacular be employed in the service, a very gradual increase of German is found even before the Reformation.

The Swedish historian, Mankell,[33] reports how on one occasion in Frankfurt on the Main, a monk holding forth in Latin was interrupted by the congregation singing a hymn in German. The same writer tells of an instance in Lübeck where the priest ". . . as was his custom began to pray for the dead in Latin, when two boys burst out in *Ach Gott von Himmel, sieh darein,* with the congregation joining in and continuing to the end."

The process of eliminating Latin from the evangelical service was very slow. The choir continued singing in Latin up through

---

[32] 121, Vol. VI, p. 289.
[33] 23, Vol. I, p. 188.

the time of Bach in the eighteenth century, interspersing their offerings with selections in German. The transition as a whole from the practices of the Roman church to a peculiarly Lutheran genus occupied most of the sixteenth century. Congregational singing did not achieve eminence till the end of the century when the new harmonic and homophonic techniques in musical composition displaced the monodic and polyphonic.

MONODIC CHORALE IN SWEDEN

The pre-Reformation period

As trade developed between Sweden and the Continent, particularly with Germany, missionaries from the Roman church started their work on Swedish soil. Monasteries and nunneries were in operation by the middle of the twelfth century. As in other places, the church substituted Latin for the vernacular in public worship and Latin was also taught in the schools operated by the church. The Gregorian type of music introduced by the church, however, was entirely foreign to the Swedes who had no music which even remotely resembled the long drawn-out vocal exercises of the priests.

The change from Latin to Swedish in the service and the transition to congregational singing was slow in Sweden as we have seen was the case in Germany. Before the Reformation reached Sweden, Swedish words were intermingled with the Latin in the Roman service, such as:

> In dulci jubilo
> Sjunger på jorden bo;

and

> Efter thig längtar mig,
> Gloriosa coeli rosa.[34]

---

[34] 23, Vol. I, p. 184.

Also, the priest would sing in Latin and the congregation would sing the same in Swedish, as

Priest: *Puer natus in Bethlehem*
Congregation: *En gosse född i Bethlehem*

As the conflict between languages continued, the priests finally agreed to an arrangement whereby the priest would sing an entire stanza in Latin and then let the congregation do the same in Swedish. After this had gone on for some time the people wanted to sing the entire hymn in their own language. Eventually the priests permitted entire Swedish hymns to be sung in the morning worship on festival occasions, such as Christmas, Easter, and other major church holidays. The old custom of singing psalms in alternating Latin and Swedish lines, however, continued in use in some localities into the seventeenth century.

The Reformation movement

The outbreak of the Reformation in Germany was of immediate interest in Sweden. Events on the Continent had almost simultaneous repercussions in Sweden. The change-over from Romanism to Lutheranism was necessarily tedious and not without its difficulties. It was not until the middle of the seventeenth century that a genuinely Swedish Lutheran service was achieved.

The Reformation movement was carried on in Sweden largely by Olaus Petri (1493-1552) and Laurentius Andrae (1480-1552). Petri studied in Wittenberg with Luther and Melanchthon at the time of Luther's break with Rome. He returned to Sweden in 1518 and immediately began reform measures in his native land. In 1524 he became rector of the Church of St. Nicholas in Stockholm where he was in a position to wield a great influence. With the ascension of Gustaf I to the throne in 1523, Petri found an ally in the cause of Protestantism who made it easier to carry out reform measures. Gustaf was interested not only in the cause of the Reformation but also in music. He "with earnestness advanced the cause of the Reformation in Sweden, accepted the church folk song introduced by Luther although changed from its original rhythm. The chorales were in this form accepted for the Swedish service," writes Mankell.[35] The number of organs in Sweden also increased considerably under Gustaf's reign.

The first son of Gustaf I, Erik XIV, tended to follow Calvinism rather than Lutheranism. The result was that less emphasis was placed on church music since this was of slight importance in the early Calvinistic service.

The decisive step which broke the power of Rome in Sweden was taken at the meeting of the *Riksdag* in Våsterås in June, 1527. A meeting of leading churchmen in Orebo two years later decided against numerous practices of the Roman church, including the use of the Latin mass.

As in Germany and the other Scandinavian countries, a wealth of religious folk music existed amongst the common people. This was the real foundation upon which their church music was to be built.

Early Lutheran hymnody

The first Swedish Lutheran hymnal was published in 1526, presumably by Olaus Petri. No copies are known to exist. A few fragmentary pages of a second hymnal published in 1530 were found in 1871. The exact number of hymns in either of these is not known because no complete copies have been pre-

---

[35] 23, Vols. II-III, p. 238.

served. The 1530 publication contained at least ten hymns. All but three of these are from German song books published between 1524-1529.[36] While there is no proof that Petri produced any of these early hymnals, neither is there proof to the contrary. Considering the zeal he put into his work there can be little doubt that he was directly connected with the work of publishing hymns for his people. It is not unlikely that even in those first years of his work as a reformer he took time to write a few hymns which would be more particularly appropriate for his people than any translations could be.

That Olaus Petri did contribute at least one hymn to a third publication in 1536 seems certain. This hymnal contained forty-four hymns, derived largely from the Low-German hymnals of Speratus and Slüter.[37] Bergendoff points out that of the forty-four hymns in the collection, twenty-four appear to be translations from Speratus' hymnal of 1526.[38] He states further that thirty-one of the hymns in Slüter's book of 1531 (it contained 112 hymns) agree wholly or, in the case of a few, in part, with the hymns in the Swedish publication. Luther's *Ein feste Burg* is one of the hymns included. A few are from Latin sources.

Laurentius Petri, a brother of Olaus and often referred to as the "father of Swedish hymnody," issued several additional editions of Olaus' hymnal after the latter's death in 1552. A hymnal of 1567 is generally accepted as being quite entirely the work of Laurentius. It contained about a hundred hymns of which about forty were new and likely translated by the editor from Danish, German, and Latin sources. Another edition of this work was issued in 1572, being combined with four small collections of religious poetry. Other editions followed, printed in

---

[36] 7, pp. 159, 160, 162.
[37] See Appendix.
[38] 7, p. 163.

Stockholm and Leipzig in 1586 and in Stockholm and Lübeck in 1594. A revised edition of the earlier hymnals was issued in Stockholm in 1601, with subsequent issues in succeeding years. The hymnbooks were used mainly by the minister and the cantor.

With literacy at a low level, the people had to be taught the hymns more or less by rote. Music from the Roman church naturally played a part also in the early Swedish Lutheran service. Hymns, sequences, and graduals were translated into Swedish and sung by the congregation in the service.

The Swedish Mass, like Luther's German Mass, included the singing of hymns by the congregation. These apparently did not go with the Communion service but with the sermon. Later on, in 1571, Laurentius Petri, then Archbishop of Uppsala, listed six chorales which could be sung as substitutes for the Latin introits. Luther's Credo had replaced the old Credo in 1536. The old Sanctus and Agnus Dei were displaced by metrical versions of the same texts by Decius, a German writer.

The meeting of the *Riksdag* at Västerås in 1527 severed the last *official* ties with Rome but the Reformation was not finally established in Sweden until it adopted the Confession of Augsburg at the synod in Uppsala in 1593. Music of the Roman church continued in use in some Swedish churches until the middle of the seventeenth century. With the awakening of a greater national consciousness during this period, all foreign languages were being systematically driven out and with them, the music of the Roman church.

The development of a native musical culture in the northern countries was a slow process. Denmark served as a channel through which music from the Continent reached the Scandinavian peninsula. Among the musical publications which found their way into Sweden toward the close of the sixteenth century was Hans Thomissön's *Salmebog* and Nils Jesperson's *Gradual,* both from Denmark. Many melodies from these books were adopted by the Swedes.

The Swedish historian, Mankell points out that some of the early Swedish hymns were translations of German hymns which were in turn translations of hymns which had originally been brought to the Continent by Norsemen at the time of the Vikings.[39] These people had settled in the Normandy area and their music and hymn literature had been absorbed by the Normans. Some of these were taken over by the German reformers and now at the time of the Reformation movement came back to Sweden as German chorales.

MONODIC CHORALE IN DENMARK AND NORWAY

The pre-Reformation period

The formation of the Union of Calmar in 1397 put Denmark, Norway, Sweden, and Iceland under a single monarch. The dissolution of this union in 1523 created Sweden's independence from the other countries and resulted in the formation of a new union between Norway, Iceland, and Denmark under Denmark's king. Final arrangements for this new union were completed in 1537. Because of these ties, the church music of Norway and Denmark can be considered together until 1814 when Norway was removed from Danish rule.

The Reformation came to Denmark through the so-called "Count's War," which began with the death of Christian II in 1533. This war was fought between a Catholic, Christopher of Oldenburg, and Christian III who had become a follower of the evangelical movement. It ended in 1536 with the capture

---

[39] 23, Vol. I, pp. 193, 194.

of Copenhagen by Christian III. As a result of this victory in arms, Norway and Denmark severed their bonds with the Roman church.

Popular Christian hymns were to be found in Denmark well before the Reformation period. Many of these hymns and melodies from the Roman period were revised and continued in use in the evangelical churches. Claus Mortensen's *Det kristelige Messeembede,* published in 1528, contained some hymns. A supplement was released soon after. In 1529, Arvid Pedersen published these collections in one volume. Simultaneously a small volume was prepared by Hans Tausen and Jørgen Sadolin. The *Malmø Salmebogen,* issued in about 1531, contained all earlier collections and became the common hymnal for the evangelical church in Denmark until replaced by Hans Tausen's hymnal in 1544. Both the Malmø and Tausen hymnals contained melodies.

Early Lutheran hymnody

The first hymnal prepared specifically for the Lutheran service in Denmark was Hans Thomissön's *Psalmebog,* published in 1569. Melodies for each hymn were included in this publication. This, together with the earlier editions of Mortensen's hymnal, constituted the hymnody of the Danish-Norwegian Lutherans for more than a century. The king commanded that Thomissön's hymnal be used in all churches, requesting that in each church one copy be secured with a chain for the use of the *klokker,* or cantor. The hymnal contained 268 selections, some of which were written by Thomissön and other contemporary hymnists, others were translations from earlier German publications and again others were native hymns which had previously come into use, many of them found in Mortensen's book.

Thomissön, in issuing his hymnal, quoted from one of Luther's prefaces to show that the hymns should have particular significance for Danish and Norwegian Lutherans.

Representative of the melodies which Thomissön borrowed from the German publications are the following:[40]

KOM HEDNINGERS FRELSER SAND

This was taken from the German hymn *Nun kom der Heidenheiland* by Luther, which, in turn, was a translation of the Latin hymn, *Veni redemptor Gentium*. The above melody is almost identical to that found in the *Erfurt Enchiridion* of 1524.

CHRISTUM WI SKULLE LOFFUE NU

Chri - stum wi skul - le loff - ue nu /
Ma - ri - ae Sön den re - ne Jom - fru /
Saa vi - - je som so - - len off -
uer - skin / Be - kien - de wi JE -
sum en HEr - re al - - leen.

---

[40] Taken from 34, pp. 7, 8.

This was taken from the German *Christum wir sollen loben schon* which Luther again had borrowed from a Latin source, *A solis ortus cardine.* It bears resemblance to the *Erfurt Enchiridion* of 1524 and Klug's hymnal of 1535. The following melodies are examples of native Danish music which Thomissön used:[41]

CHRIST HAFFUE LOFF

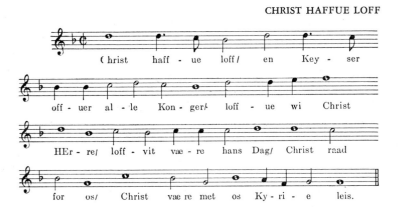

JEG VIL MIG HERREN LOFFUE

---

[41] 34, pp. 9, 10.

A careful study of these examples will reveal two distinct characteristics: those of German origin show definite Gregorian features with notes mostly of equal value, while those of Danish folk music origin show a buoyant spirit, having a more pronounced rhythmic movement. In these two styles we find the bone of contention which developed in the northern countries between two musical factions and which has continued down to our own time.

The Scandinavian countries had not developed a musical tradition and culture of their own strong enough to withstand the musical styles promoted by German musicians who came in with the Reformation and to a great extent dominated the music of the church. The struggle between imported and native music continued until such a time that musicians could be trained in their home countries under teachers who themselves had helped shape an indigenous musical culture.

Thomissön's hymnal had a glorious career. An enlarged version was issued in 1586. No changes were then made until 1634 when Bishop H. P. Resen brought out an improved edition with minor changes in both texts and melodies. Meanwhile, a number of other collections of hymns had been prepared, some of which were widely used, such as the *Haandbogen* of 1578, *Vandrebogen* of about 1591, and a hymnal by Anders Arrebos of 1623.

A very significant contribution to early Lutheran church music in Denmark was Nils Jesperson's *Gradual,* published in 1573. From the preface we learn that it was to have been released at the same time as Thomissön's *Salmebog* in 1569. The *Gradual* contained the melodies for the hymnals in use at that time. The sixty Danish hymns in this work are arranged according to the Sundays in the church year, with hymns for each high mass (*Höjmesse*) and a few evening songs, songs for prayer, for the bridal mass, and so on. In addition to the Danish hymns are sixty-two Latin introits, thirteen Latin sequences, four Latin responses, and several miscellaneous items. Some of the hymns are translations from the German, such as the *Aus tiefer Not, Christ lag in Todesbanden, Isaiah dem Propheten,* and *Ein feste Burg.* The following are musical excerpts from this interesting work of over 460 pages:[42]

J TRO ALLESAMMEN PAA EN GUD

J   tro   allesammen   paa en Gud

GUDS LAM WSKYLDIG

VOR GUD HAN ER SAA FAST EN BORG

---

[42] These selections are from pages 11, 18, and 388 respectively. Thomissön had the same version of the first example.

Jesperson's *Gradual* was designed more for the city churches and for school use. Thomissön's hymnal was used mostly in rural areas.

While the German Lutherans had accepted a number of Gregorian melodies as chorale tunes and had adopted Gregorian characteristics of style in their own individual contributions, the Scandinavians found it quite impossible to wed their language to the style of the Roman chant. The ancient chants grew out of the Latin words with which they had been associated from earliest times. To set other words to these chants was found quite impossible. Neither were their native composers in a position as yet to supply melodies for the new hymns. Because of this they relied, for church music, on their own stores of folk melodies. No doubt one reason why Jesperson found it necessary to include a number of Latin introits, sequences, responses, and other selections from the Roman service was because of the lack of suitable music for similar selections in the Danish language.

To counteract the continued usage of Latin in the hymnody of the church, Bishop Thomas Kingo (1634-1703) of Slanger-up, ushered in the first genuine Danish period. He aimed to have the complete service in Danish no matter what happened. Because of his talent and great influence, Kingo became known as the first great Danish hymn writer. His hymns are particularly indigenous to his homeland and embody expressions of sentiment native to his people.

Kingo published his *Aandelige Sjunge-Koor* in two volumes in 1674 and 1681. These volumes were widely used. Part I reached its sixth edition in 1694 and Part II was reissued in 1686. After his death, both volumes were issued several times. In his preface to Part I he defends his point in having the hymns sung to native Danish melodies, many of which were from secular sources, by saying that his predecessors had done the same. It appears, however, that his forefathers had drawn on *folkevisor,* a near relative of church song, whereas Kingo used *selskabsvisor,* which were purely secular melodies. In his preface he also states, "Do not let it seem strange or absurd that I have set these spiritual morning and evening songs together with the sacred and edifying King David's psalms under some melodies which otherwise are sung by many with worldly words."

In 1683, Kingo was asked to prepare a common hymnal for the church. This resulted in *Danmarks og Norges Kirkers forordnede Salmebog,* but it was met with a storm of disapproval because of its cold rationalism and because it contained so many of his own hymns. A revised version was then prepared and issued in 1699 and has been generally known as *Kingo's Hymnal.* This remained in use for many generations, subject to several revisions and enlargements.

In 1699 also, Kingo published a *Gradual,* which, in contrast to his music for *Aandelige Sjunge-Koor,* represents the older type of church music. This work contained melodies for hymnals then in popular use, and replaced *Thomissön's* hymnal which was now scarcely to be found in the churches.

From the introduction to Kingo's *Gradual* we call attention to what he has to say about the singing of Gregorian chant in the Scandinavian churches:

. . . from the time of Pope Gregory the Great who introduced his Gregorian songs which the common people here in the North and other neighboring lands and kingdoms were unable to understand, and its mis-use came to the point where the ordinary man should read "The Lord's Prayer" together with the angel-greeting or Ava Maria in Latin, although the poor people themselves never knew what they either sang or read.

The older melodies as found in Thomissön were to undergo considerable change in the hands of the aggressive Kingo. Even though his *Gradual* appears to be a compromise between the older church music drawn from Roman and German sources and the native Danish melodies for which he had a strong preference, Kingo took the liberty of altering the old melodies to put them into a more varied rhythmic movement. For example, Jesperson's first melody on page 39 was given this version by Kingo:[43]

tro   al - le - sam - men   paa   en   Gud

The following melody in Thomissön's hymnal[44]

Oc   loff - ue   vor   HEr - re   i

al - len   stad   Ky - ri - e - leis.

appeared in this version in Kingo's *Gradual:*[45]

Og   lov - ve   vor   HEr - re   i

al - len   stad.   Ky - ri - e - e leis.

---

[43] 81, p. 15.
[44] 34, p. 16.
[45] 81, p. 18.

Kingo had a decided preference for triple meter, as shown by the following well-known melody:[46]

SOM HJORTEN MED TÖRST BEFANGEN

Melodies of such waltzlike characteristics are too superficial to endure in the realm of serious church music.

Kingo's version of Luther's *Ein feste Burg* as given in his *Gradual* is as follows:[47]

VOR GUD HAN ER SAA FAST EN BORG

---

[46] 81, p. 99.
[47] 81, p. 131.

43

Melodic and rhythmic alterations such as these were not necessarily unique. Since the first evangelical hymnals were published in Germany, editors have felt themselves qualified to make whatever alterations the text or music might need to meet their own wishes. Instead of discarding melodies which did not meet with their approval, they resorted to a reckless kind of carving which over a period of a few generations often found the melody bearing only a general resemblance to the original.

2

Early Homophonic
and Harmonic Techniques
1586-1680

POET-COMPOSERS AND POETS IN GERMANY

The number of chorale melodies increased considerably in the second half of the sixteenth century with many of the hymn writers supplying also the melodies for their hymns. This had been done by Nikolaus Decius and Nikolaus Hermann earlier in the century and their contributions remained a significant part of the sixteenth century hymn literature and are still in use today. Decius (d. 1541), a Bavarian preacher and musician, supplied metrical versions of the Sanctus, Gloria in Excelsis, and the Agnus Dei, to which he also gave musical settings. Hermann, (d. 1561) for many years cantor at Joachimsthal in Bohemia, was perhaps the greatest poet-composer of the period. His polyphonic compositions were written for two voices.

Another great poet-musician was Philip Nicolai (d. 1608) whose religious treatise *Freudenspiegel des ewigen Lebens,* published in 1598, had four hymns appended, including the famous *Wachet auf! ruft uns die Stimme,* and *Wie schön leuchtet der Morgenstern* which have remained universal favorites. For these immortal hymns, Nicolai wrote the melodies as well as the words.

Other prominent hymn writers of this period include Nikolaus Selnecker, Bartholomaeus Ringwald, Martin Behm, Martin Moller, Ludwig Helmbold, and Martin Schalling. Selnecker, a pupil of Melanchthon, was one of the framers of the Formula of Concord, the adoption of which resolved the differences and controversies that were threatening the new church. He wrote about 150 hymns, a number of which remain in use.

The first century of the Reformation produced hymns of an objective type, hymns of praise and adoration and what might well be called the "doctrinal" songs of the Reformation. The period of the Thirty Years War (1618-1648) stimulated a more subjective type of sacred poetry resulting in the *Kreutz-* and *Trostlieder* (songs of the cross and of consolation), and the *Erbauungslieder* (songs of edification). God was not only the Supreme Being who was to be worshiped and adored, he was also their comfort and help in time of affliction. The hymns of this period ring with a sincerity and devoutness found for the first time. This period of Christian self-consciousness was to lead eventually into the Pietistic movement at the close of the seventeenth century. Hymn writers of this period include Valerius Herberger (d. 1627), Johann Heerman (d. 1647), and Martin Rinkart (d. 1649) who wrote the immortal "Now Thank We all Our God." It was not written, however, in commemoration of the close of the war in 1648 as is often supposed. Julian[48] points out that it very likely appeared in the first edition of Rinkart's *Jesu Hertz-Büchlein* of 1636—twelve years before the war closed. It appeared in the 1663 edition of this booklet as a short table prayer.

---

[48] 115, p. 963.

Only a few of the 600 hymns of Johann Rist (d. 1667) have remained in use. Most of the melodies for his hymns were supplied by his friend, Johann Schop, who became musical director of the town council and *Kapellmeister* at Hamburg in 1621. Rist was crowned poet laureate by Emperor Ferdinand III in 1644 and became the center of the "Hamburg School," the influence of which reached out to Bremen, Lübeck, Munich, and Berlin.

Many of the hymns of Paul Gerhardt were written in the immediate postwar years. Gerhardt was pastor in Berlin and later in Lübben. He wrote a total of 123 hymns, many of which are the finest in all sacred poetry. His contributions are considered by many to be next in importance to Martin Luther's.

The technique of hymn writing on a refined poetical basis also had its beginnings in this period. The systematic efforts inaugurated by Martin Opitz, the "father of German poetry," and various literary organizations did much to improve not only the rules of poetry, with special emphasis on style, rhyme, and meter, but also improved the literary quality of the German language. This is evident in the hymns of the period in their smoother flow of well-chosen words. The crudeness so common in the early poetry of the Reformation gave way to a more refined, a more musical type of poetical expression.

The second half of the century produced such notable hymn writers as Johann Franck (d. 1677) and Georg Neumark (d. 1681), the latter winning recognition also as a composer. Rudolph Ahle (d. 1673), also made lasting contributions as a composer.

TRANSITION TO HARMONY

The close of the sixteenth century ushered in an innovation in the musical setting of the chorale which was to influence radically the future development of music. Up to this time, composers had conceived musical compositions on a horizontal plane with the musical material being spun out in several melodies performed concurrently. This type of music (polyphonic) was capable of only a limited expression and did not serve the needs of a more musically-enlightened era. The close of the century was to see the Italian opera composers discard the intricate polyphonic structure because it was totally unfit for their purpose. They adopted a homophonic style, consisting of melody with a sketchy harmonic accompaniment.

In Germany the church musicians were dissatisfied with some aspects of their music; congregational singing was still carried on in a limited manner. It became evident that both the choir and the organ had to be put to greater use in the interest of congregational singing. This required a new type of music— music which would be simple and uniform in rhythmic movement.

To meet this situation, Lukas Osiander, a pastor and at one time organist in the Frauenkirche in Nürnberg, published in that city in 1586 his *Fünfzig geistliche Lieder.* The translation of the complete title reads: "Fifty spiritual songs for four voices, set in such a way that the whole congregation can join in them." The title of this epoch-making book is self-explanatory. This was the first publication designed to unite the choir and congregation in singing the hymns. The intricate and devious weavings of polyphony were now replaced by a simple, clean-cut, *vertical* musical structure of chords. The melody was now taken from the tenor and given to the soprano as another aid in congregational singing, making it easier for the congregation to follow the melody.

Osiander's innovation was not only a remarkable step forward so far as congregational singing is concerned but also was a tremendous influence in determining the future course of church music. The rigidity of polyphony now gave way to a more elastic homophonic type of music which was to dominate the musical scene thereafter. While Osiander was not a great composer, his method was followed by others such as Eccard in his *Geistliche Lieder auff den Choral* in 1597, Gesius in his *Geistliche deutsche Lieder* in 1601, Hassler in his *Kirchengesänge* in 1608, and Vulpius in his *Gesangbuch* in 1609.

Johannes Eccard was one of the finest church composers of his time. He had studied with the great Netherland composer, Orlando di Lasso, and wrote his choir settings for five or more voices. Melchior Vulpius, cantor at Weimar, wrote chorale settings for three, four, and five voices. His hymnbooks of 1604 and 1609 contain several of his compositions. Hans Leo Hassler was one of the most outstanding composers of the period. He had studied with Andrae Gabrieli in Venice. From 1601 he was organist at the Frauenkirche in Nürnberg and was later employed at the Dresden court. Hassler wrote a great deal of both secular and sacred music. In so far as his contribution to church music is concerned, he holds the unique distinction as composer of a love song setting which has become one of the most favorite chorale melodies. The melody for *Mein G'müt ist mir verwirret* was first published in *Lustgarten* in 1601. This was a collection of "New German songs, balletti, galliards, and intrades, for four, five, and eight voices."[49] This was subsequently appropriated as a chorale melody for Paul Gerhardt's *O Haupt voll Blut und Wunden* ("O Sacred Head Now Wounded").

The work of these men, however, did not materially aid

---

[49] 70, from the full title of the book.

congregational singing since their interest was mainly in the choir. To use the choir as an organ in leading congregational singing did not prove particularly effective as will be seen later.

Another prominent musician of the period was Melchior Teschner, cantor at Fraustadt in Silesia. He wrote several fine melodies which still maintain their popularity.

Several examples from the work of these men are here given.

[50] 58, No. 4.
[51] 96, p. 41.

Hans Leo Hassler[52]

Melchior Vulpius[53]

[52] 69.
[53] 110, page 46. Each voice is on a separate staff in the original.

Comparing these numbers with earlier settings of the chorale melodies, such as those given on pages 22 and 27, one will see the contrast between these simple harmonic progressions and the elaborate interweaving of the voices in the polyphonic technique. The uniqueness of the harmonic setting at that time, however, cannot be overemphasized. This new harmonic technique was to open a new field of harmonic experimentation and radically alter the technique of every composer.

The greatest church music publication of this period was *Musae Sioniae* by Michael Prätorius, issued from 1605 to 1610. Prätorius was *Kapellmeister* to the Duke of Brunswick and later to the Elector of Saxony. He was a versatile musician and well acquainted with the Venetian, Roman, and French music of his day. His publication contains 1244 settings of chorale melodies arranged for groups from two-part choirs to quadruple four-voice choirs. His work is a collection of the best music in Germany at that time. His contribution places him as the greatest single leader in Protestant church music since Johann Walther. An example of his four-part setting follows.[54]

---

[54] 101, Part V, No. 68.

The introduction of the harmonic technique did not preclude the continuation of the polyphonic practices of the preceding period. The following is Prätorius' setting of *Ein feste Burg*.[55]

Ein fe - ste Burg ist un - - ser Gott ein

Ein fe - ste Burg - - - - - - ist un - ser Gott ein

Ein fe - ste Burg ist un - ser Gott ein

Ein fe - ste Burg - - - - - ist un - ser · Gott ein

---

[55] 101, Part VIII, No. 100.

gu - te Wehr und Waf - - - fen.

gu - te Wehr und Waf - - - fen.

gu - te - - - Wehr - - - und Waf - - - fen.

gu - - - te Wehr und Waf - - - fen.

The period of the Thirty Years War left Germany weakened musically as well as politically. The nation was so broken by strife and dissensions that any continuation of artistic development was impossible. Without a strong native group of musicians the nation lay open to a musical invasion from Italy in the south and France and the Netherlands in the west. The composers and cantors had lost contact with the great body of chorale literature which had previously developed. Now the "spiritual song" and the "spiritual aria" came into existence under Italian operatic influence, with composers devoting themselves to both sacred and secular music, making no distinction in style between the two. The true church-music composer no longer existed.

The use of the organ

The organ in the early evangelical service continued in use as had been the custom in the Roman service. There it had been used to play preludes and to give the tone to the priest or the choir, alternating with the latter in the liturgical songs and hymns—one verse being sung by the choir, followed by the same music on the organ. The organ was not used to accompany the choir and neither was it used to accompany congregational hymn singing.

The organ was therefore used independently, not as an accompaniment. In the hymn singing of the evangelical church it would be used to play a chorale, alternating with the stanzas sung by the congregation. Because it was used independently, organists gradually submitted to the temptation of playing running passages as they played preludes to the hymns and at times also played secular songs for the offertory or other occasions. Pope Clement VIII in 1600 issued orders curtailing the use of the organ in Roman churches because such evil practices had crept in. A later period was to see the organ gradually encroaching upon the musical part of the service, robbing both congregation and choir of their legitimate musical functions.

There is no reason to suppose that Luther had any interest in the organ. His voluminous writings scarcely mention the instrument and when he does, he treats it almost with scorn. The organ was more to be *tolerated* in the Lutheran service than *desired.*

The condition which made it impossible for the organ to accompany congregational singing was that no music existed for the instrument to be used for this purpose. It was necessary for the harmonic technique of musical composition to develop before music could be written for the organ for this purpose. While Osiander's type of musical structure made it possible for the congregation to sing along with the choir in the hymns, this was not a cure-all for the ills of congregational singing. The small choir found it difficult to support the congregation in hymn singing. The technique introduced by Osiander, however, brought forth a type of music which would now make it possible for the organ to lend its support to congregational singing.

One of the pronounced trends of the postwar period was the emphasis placed upon organ building and organ playing. Instrumental music in general was now for the first time coming into its own. Organs were often built as community projects and organ dedications became great celebrations. The period following the middle of the seventeenth century was to see the organ gain such prominence as to tip the balance between organ music and congregational singing with the organ coming out on top. The church now was the only place where elaborate music could be performed. The courts with their orchestras and choirs were so depleted after the war that they were no longer in a position to promote an elaborate musical program.

Not all developments in organ music in this period can be considered gain, however. Michael Prätorius, a prominent composer of serious music, called for such gadgets as a cuckoo, the sound of a bumble bee, the bleating of a goat, and the roll of a drum in his organ compositions. On occasion the congregation was edified by having the organist set into motion a sun and the morning star. On Ascension Day he pulled a picture of Christ to the ceiling of the church to the accompaniment of trombone stops and lutes.

One of the early publications written for the organist for accompanying was Johann Hermann Schein's *Cantional*, published in 1627. This publication contained melodies and figured bass for "organists, instrumental players and lutenists," and was used to accompany the choir. Schein was cantor at the St. Thomas School in Leipzig, a position later held by J. S. Bach.

The transition from the use of the choir to the organ for accompanying congregational singing was made gradually as the technique of harmonic musical composition grew. The Hamburg *Melodienbuch* of 1604 proclaimed "Each Christian can with good courage lift up and noisily use his modest untrained voice and from now on is no longer the fifth wheel but the fourth and good wheel of the wagon of music to the laud and praise of God's Name."[56]

The first satisfactory organ book for accompanying congregational singing was published in 1650 by Samuel Scheidt, a pupil of the great Netherland composer and organist, Sweelinck. Scheidt is by some referred to as the "father of German organ music." He prepared his Tabulature Book while serving as organist at Halle. The work contained 112 settings of 100 melodies in use at that time. The publication helped establish him as a leader in organ music in central and northern Europe, attracting students from much of this territory, among them the future great Buxtehude.

An example of Scheidt's musical setting in modern notation follows:[57]

[56] 26, Vol. II, p. 39.
[57] 94, No. 2.

It was not long after Scheidt's publication was issued that the organ displaced entirely the choir as the leader of congregational singing. By this time, too, the organ was a well-developed musical instrument.

One of the greatest musical publications to come out of this period, and one of the most influential in any period, was Johann Crüger's *Praxis pietatis melica,* probably published in 1644. This noteworthy publication had forty-three editions by 1733. The musical setting consisted of melody and bass. His *Geistliche Kirchen-Melodien* published at about the same time had a setting for four voices and two instruments. Following is a setting in four parts of the old Latin hymn, *A solis ortus cardine,* by Crüger:[58]

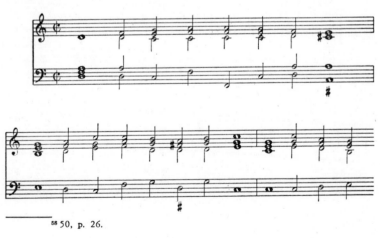

[58] 50, p. 26.

While cantor at the St. Nicolaus Church in Berlin from 1622 till his death in 1662, Crüger occupied an influential position in the field of church music. Many of the lyrics of Paul Gerhardt are sung to musical settings by Crüger.

Music notation

The practice of modernizing the notation of music throughout this period was apparently a slow process. The following two melodies are taken from a hymnal published in Dresden in 1656.[59]

---

[59] 53, Nos. 39 and 725. This is a large work of about 1300 pages.

To facilitate reading, all selections have been given in modern notation. The music of this period, and even up through the eighteenth century, was written in the C clef for the upper parts while the F clef was used for the lower. In music consisting of only two staffs, the upper staff generally has the C clef on the first line. Where each voice part is given on a separate staff, the top voice will be in the C clef on the first line, the second voice, C clef on the third line, and the third voice (tenor), with the C clef on the fourth line.[60]

Ornamentation

The following excerpt from a hymn melody from a publication dated 1676,[61] is given to show the ornamental type of melody which crept in during this period and came to be a prominent characteristic under Pietism. This came about through the general secularization of church music which was going on, dominated to some extent by the aria of the Italian opera, the popularity of which was sweeping over central Europe at this time.

---

[60] Compare with examples on pages 22 and 25.
[61] From the *Nürnbergisches Gesang-buch* of 1676. Copied from 34, p. 16.

THE HARMONIC CHORALE IN SWEDEN

Foreign influence

Because the Scandinavian countries as yet had not developed a strong musical culture of their own the musical scene was dominated by foreigners, largely Germans. Germany became the source of music for the church. Georg Weber, a German, published the first part of his *Geistliche Lieder* in Stockholm in 1640 during his stay there. Crüger's *Praxis* was widely used in Sweden before the close of the seventeenth century. Scheidt's *Tabulatur* was widely used in Uppsala, in the St. Nikolai Church and in the German church in Stockholm and in Våsterås. Mention has already been made of the Danish publications used in Sweden: Thomissön's *Psalmebog* and Jesperson's *Gradual.* Kingo's *Aandelige Sjunge-Koor* came out in a Swedish edition in 1689.

Swedish publications

Many collections of hymns appeared after 1600 which were in use throughout the century. In 1620 the enchiridions of Petrus Rudbeck and his brother John, Bishop of Våsterås, were published. These included melodies together with the hymns. In 1643 the *Svenska Uppsala Psalmboken* was issued for use throughout the entire country. It contained no music so that the older hymnals with melodies still had to be consulted. *Psalme-prover,* a hymnal with melodies, was published in Uppsala in 1689 by Arrhenius. A number of the new hymns in this collection were translations from the German.

German musicians held prominent positions in Sweden both as church organists and as court musicians. They gave concerts of German music, with compositions by Prätorius, Heinrich Grimm, and Heinrich Schütz given prominence. The German church in Stockholm where Andreas Düben served as organist was a center of many musical activities. He had come from Germany under Gustaf Adolph's reign and had been engaged as organist at the court. Ogier, a member of the French diplomatic corps in Stockholm, wrote as early as 1635 in his diary about "an evening in the German church where Andreas Düben was organist, performing music for choir, orchestra, and organ, which lasted till late at night."[62]

At this time, the position of organist was usually inherited. In due time, Düben's son, Gustaf, born in Stockholm in 1624, occupied his father's positions at both the court and the church. As was generally the case, however, he was called on to do more than just play the organ since he would "play the violin by note for dances and accompany on the violoncello and also be experienced on some wind instrument . . . so as to be able to instruct pupils and help the children with music at festive occasions in and out of church."[63]

Gustaf Düben was a good friend of the Lübeck organists, Tunder and Buxtehude. He was held in high regard by musicians throughout the country and drew many skilled performers and composers to the Swedish capital. His best period was from 1660-1670. By 1680 his health prevented him from participating actively in musical affairs. He supplied the melodies for a hymnal, *Odae Sveticae,* prepared by Samuel Columbus and published in 1674. Columbus was also a German and had been called in 1628 as professor at Uppsala.

In the early seventeenth century the greater share of the singing in the church service was done by the choir, with the congregation taking part in the more familiar hymns. Such

[62] 24, p. 432.
[63] 24, p. 432.

prestige led to carelessness by the choir with the result that, as congregational singing later developed to the point of prominence, the choir had to mend its ways to regain its position in the church service. By the middle of the century church leaders tried to maintain a satisfactory balance between the congregation and choir. In the cities the school children sang in the choir. But in the country, where no choir was available, the cantor was to stand in the middle of the church and "hold the simple and unlearned together in the melody."[64]

THE HARMONIC CHORALE IN DENMARK AND NORWAY

What was true in Sweden held good also in Denmark and Norway. Native progress on a harmonic basis did not start until the publication of a chorale book in Denmark by the German organist F. C. Breitendich, organist at the St. Nicolai Church in Copenhagen, in 1764. As in Sweden, the larger churches with organs used publications available for that instrument while the many churches without organs sang under the leadership of the cantor, selecting the melodies from the various enchiridions, hymnbooks, and graduals which were available.[65]

---

[64] 30, p. 114.

[65] The discussion of Thomas Kingo's music, already given, belongs chronologically in this period. Since no harmony was involved, it was discussed under the monodic music of the earlier period.

3

The End of An Era

1680-1750

THE GERMAN CHORALE

The Pietistic movement

The tendency toward a more subjective type of Christian thinking which developed during the grievous years of the Thirty Years War continued into a strong Pietistic movement later in the century. Jakob Spener, pastor of St. Nicolai Church in Berlin, became the leader of this movement. The sterile scholasticism and cold objectivity of late sixteenth century Lutheranism was not meeting the needs of Lutherans of the seventeenth century. This movement is well illustrated in the hymns of the period, particularly in the frequent use of the singular pronouns "I," "my," "me," in contrast to the plural forms of "we" and "our" in the earlier Reformation period. The former represent the individual's relation to his God, the latter the group, or congregational approach. The following hymns can be taken as representative of these two modes of religious thinking.

ALL GLORY BE TO GOD ON HIGH

All glory be to God on high,
Who hath our race befriended

To us no harm shall now come nigh,
The strife at last is ended.
God showeth His good will to men,
And peace shall reign on earth again;
O thank Him for His goodness.
                    —N. Decius, 1526.
                    Trans. C. Winkworth

JESUS, MY CAPTAIN, TO VICTORY LEAD ME

Jesus, my Captain, to victory lead me,
Swiftly the powers of darkness draw near.
Thou who from Satan's dominion hath freed me,
Lend me Thy help and allay all my fear.
Seeing the tempter would cunningly sift me,
Do Thou in mercy sustain and uplift me.
                    —J. Schroeder, c. 1666.
                    Trans. H. Brueckner

Pietism was not friendly toward art of any kind. Art was regarded as being "of the world." The continued development of music during this period was seriously threatened. The spirit of subjectivism which characterized the Pietistic movement deserted the rugged, forceful melodies of the Reformation and used instead a freer-moving Italian operatic type of melody. The sentiments of the Pietistic hymn writers could not be sung to the virile melodies of the Reformation. The use of triple meter became common, often resulting in a waltzlike movement. This was a countermove to the type of melody which the Lutheran chorale had inherited from the Gregorian plain song where the notes tended to be of equal durational value. Neither did it have much in common with folk melodies which had been used in both Germany and the Scandinavian countries. The more staid German music was now subjected to the rapidly spreading ornamental Italian music of the period which was considered more "artistic" than the German. The true chorale melody seemed incapable of further development. Spitta says that "... in pietistic circles nothing was encouraged but 'spiritual songs' of the narrowest type, which followed the verse as closely and simply as possibly."[66] Composers merely "set music" to religious texts and gave little thought to the serious composition of church music. Together with the lessened interest in church music came the inevitable cut in appropriations for music and services by musicians in the churches. Cognizance must also be taken of the fact that in the eighteenth century artistic expression found a better medium through literature than through music. Music in the church was steadily losing ground while secular music, notably Italian opera, was exerting a tremendous influence. Hymn singing in the congregations lost its vigor as "the 'spiritual songs' which displaced the magnificent treasure of chorale melodies led to the arbitrarily set, gloomy, and dragging congregational singing which was a caricature of the sturdy and lively chorales of the heroic age of the Reformation."[67]

Pietism's emphasis upon the individual resulted in the preparation of hymnals designed to meet the needs of every person and every occasion. A Mecklenburg pastor made up a collection of songs for 147 different professions in 1716. Lang relates that in 1737 a Saxon clergyman published a "universal songbook in which songs were to be found for christenings, marriages, and other family events, others appropriate for difficult lawsuits, for lameness, blindness, deafness, or for the affliction of having too many children, and for noblemen, ministers, officials, lawyers, barbers, bakers, fishermen, teamsters, merchants' apprentices, and many other professions," and requested songs for "clowns, tight-rope walkers, magicians, thieves, and rogues."[68]

---

[66] 119, Vol. I, pp. 362, 363.
[67] 19, p. 107.
[68] 19, p. 470.

The nature of the music promoted by Pietism led to an emphasis on dramatic choruses, arias with obbligato instrumental parts such as were used in Italian opera, and recitatives of considerable length. Worshipers who found it tiresome to listen to such music were encouraged to read their prayer books during the performance of the music.

Increased use of the organ

The laws of compensation seemed to be in operation in so far as church music in this period is concerned. Congregational singing gradually diminished while the organ became more and more important. ". . . the instrument strove to display all its wealth and power, the voices became more and more silent," says Spitta.[69] He continues, ". . . the organist . . . would not refrain from embroidering on the melody an arbitrary ornamentation, altering its organism by interposing his own fancies." Jacob Adlung, a noted theologian, scholar, and musician, wrote that "when so many play as loud as they can, to perform whole passages, intermingled with regular closes, beginning quickly, and then again leaving off slowly, so that either the congregation sing on all out of order, or else must wait too long—it can hardly be said to be the finest performance in this best of worlds."[70]

The organists soon took up the practice of supplying interludes which had become a favorite device with many cantors. The Swedish historian, Mankell, cites the following illustration of how the cantor would come in with a vocal exercise between two lines of the chorale:[71]

---

[69] 119, Vol. I, p. 593.
[70] Quoted from Spitta, 119, Vol. I, p. 594.
[71] 95, Vol. I, p. 261.

This type of decoration came to be known as the *Zwischenspiel* in organ music and remained in use for a considerable time and is to be found in some early German-American chorale books.

The following is an example of organ music of the period, used to accompany congregational singing:[72]

[72] 104, No. 7.

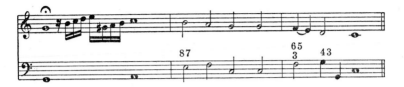

These interludes came either at the end of complete stanzas or at the end of verse lines as in the above example. "Interludes," says Spitta, "are mere empty vehicles for the display of ignorance and barbarism . . ."[73] The German composer, Georg Weber who spent some time in Stockholm, said that "All training for the so-called 'invention' of the *Zwischenspiel* is a hint of performing something crazy."[74]

Publications

One of the earliest important publications in this period was the *Andächtigen Seelen geistliches Brand- und Gantz-Opfer* published in Leipzig in 1697. It contained over 5,000 hymns.

The greatest publication of the period was Johann Freylinghausen's *Gesangbuch* of 1704. This was followed by a new collection in 1714. The two were combined in 1741, forming a collection of 1,600 hymns with over 600 melodies with figured bass. Freylinghausen's hymnal was used extensively and passed through a number of editions. The effect of Pietism is clearly noticeable in the treatment of the music as well as the texts. The older chorale melodies were too rigid for the Pietistic poets so the melodies had to be enlivened or new ones provided. The following example is a good illustration of how this was done.[75] The following melody in the Nürnberg *Evangelisches Choral Buch* of 1731:

---

[73] 119, Vol. I, p. 594.
[74] 23, Vol. I, p. 263.
[75] 66, No. 1131.

No. 385

was given this version in Freylinghausen:

No. 490

while the *Wirtembergische Land-Gesangbuch* of 1799 has this version of the same melody:

No. 104

which shows the continued use of the Freylinghausen style.

Following is the complete setting of Luther's *Ein feste Burg* as given in Freylinghausen:[76]

No. 1131

---

[76] Freylinghausen's hymnal gives the soprano part and the "figured bass" from which the organist would develop the complete harmonization. See Appendix for a solution of figured bass.

The ancient plain song type of melody written by Luther had to undergo considerable alterations to meet the taste of Freylinghausen.

Concerning the Freylinghausen type of melody, the orthodox theological faculty in Wittenberg in 1714 complained of "The running and dancing manner whereby the heart was set into violent motion, yes, almost in a fury, which fought against the seriousness and sublimity of the matter, against the customs of the evangelical church. . ."[77]

J. S. Bach

It was perhaps a trick of fate that Lutheranism's greatest composer should have done his work in a period such as this. Interest in church music had already begun to wane before Johann Sebastian Bach came upon the scene. "Pietism," says Spitta, "had finished off good church music so that when Bach came he had little to work with."[78]

When Bach applied for the position at the *Thomasschule* in Leipzig, some congregations were singing hymns without organ

[77] 20, p. 120.
[78] 119, Vol. II, p. 115.

accompaniment and large parts of the liturgy were being sung in Latin. Spitta comments that "The custom, which was becoming more and more general, of accompanying the congregational singing throughout on the organ, had not yet come into use at Leipzig."[79] Quoting further from Spitta, "Even on festal and ordinary Sundays, the 'sermon' hymn at least was always sung without accompaniment," although in 1755 at the festival of the Reformation this custom was broken down. Choirs also as a rule had been singing without accompaniment. But in 1717 Mattheson was prompted to complain, "Where are the vocalists who used to sing without instruments, even without a bass, whether clavier or organ?"[80] In Leipzig, motets by the choir had been accompanied customarily by cornets and trombones up through the sixteenth century to the time of Bach. Unaccompanied choral singing had not been the common practice in the evangelical churches. At the time of Bach the organ accompanied all choral works.

While living in Leipzig where he taught at the St. Thomas School, Bach collected about 240 currently used chorale melodies. Some of these were copied by his pupils together with his own harmonizations and used by them in accompanying congregational singing. Very few of these have come down to us.

Bach was not very much interested in writing hymn tunes. He felt there were too many big things to be done. It is likely that he contributed twenty-nine melodies for a little-used hymnal prepared by Schemelli, primarily for home worship. Included in this group is the now famous *Komm Süsser Tot*. "Bach could hardly have intended them as melodies suitable for public worship," says Spitta. "They were sacred arias . . .

---

[79] 119, Vol. II, p. 278.
[80] 119, Vol. II, p. 279.

not more than five of them have been included in any of the later choral collections."[81] Bach's greatest contribution to chorale literature did not lie in writing chorale melodies but rather in the 371 four-part harmonizations he made of chorale melodies and the many chorale preludes he wrote for organ.

Schweitzer[82] observes that congregational singing at the time of Bach was not likely very important. The organist and choir had the musical parts of the service pretty well to themselves. "Not until the concert style of music was banished from the service, in the generation after Bach, and the town choirs that had been allotted to the churches ceased to exist," states Schweitzer, "did congregational singing become the characteristic and sole service-music of the Protestant church." The "town choirs" here referred to were the choirs trained by the "town musician," which sang in the churches. The leader, not necessarily chosen because of qualifications as a church musician, was engaged by the town. Hymnbooks were not commonly used by the members of the congregation. They were supposed to know by memory the hymns for each Sunday of the church year.

From the time of Luther to that of Bach, masses by Protestant and Catholic composers alike had been performed in the Lutheran service. In Leipzig in Bach's time, not only the choir numbers were in Latin, but even the reading of the Epistle and Gospel. Bach also wrote a mass, at first only the first two movements, the Kyrie and the Gloria, which had been retained by the Lutherans in the musical mass. The remaining movements were added later, making it a work of concert proportions.

Still greater confusion was brought into the picture by the

---

[81] 119, Vol. II, p. 112. It should be noted in this connection that the English historian, Charles Sanford Terry, published in 1922 a book entitled *J. S. Bach's Original Hymn-Tunes for Congregational use,* including twenty-six hymns. This is in disagreement with Schweitzer's position.

[82] 118, Vol. I, p. 39.

professional musicians engaged by the churches. Cantors, who were usually church-trained men—often future pastors or teachers—were now being replaced by prominent musicians. Some of these, coming from operatic and orchestral positions, were now asked to furnish music for the church! Some musicians worked for both Protestant and Catholic churches. Rather than being "church musicians" they were "musicians in the church," and very often frustrated musicians—those who had not made good in opera or on the concert stage.

Under these conditions the significance of the chorale decreased together with interest in good church music. Bach's own sons had little interest in the chorale tradition. Most of his music remained unpublished until its discovery by Mendelssohn a hundred years later. By the time of his death in 1750 not only music, but theology as well, had fallen under the ban of rationalism. Genuine church music lay dormant, awaiting an awakening which is still in progress.

Chorale examples

Two examples published in this period are here given.[83]

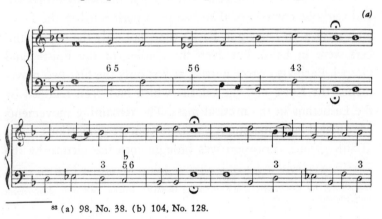

---

[83] (a) 98, No. 38. (b) 104, No. 128.

It is quite apparent that the decorative style of Freylinghausen is continued in these examples.

THE SWEDISH CHORALE

Tendency toward uniformity

Toward the middle of the seventeenth century, a pronounced movement toward unity in church practice in Sweden was under way. This involved not only the state church but also the German church in Stockholm as well. "Similarity in church customs, ceremonies, and church song became the watchword of the period," says Norlind.[84] The practices and music carried over from the Middle Ages gave way to the newer Reformation forms and practices. This step is plainly seen in the church order

---

[84] 30, p. 107.

of 1693 and the *Psalm- och Evangelieboken* of 1695 which embodied many of the revisions which came into use as a genuine Swedish Lutheran service evolved.

The *Svenska Uppsala Psalmboken* of 1643 had been prepared for the purpose of achieving uniformity in the church service. But it contained no melodies and the older publications with melodies, such as Rudbeck's *Enchiridion* had to be used. A pastor's handbook published in 1693 had notation but this was solely for the pastor's use. "One therefore continued mostly referring to the hand-written mass- and chorale-books," says Norlind,[85] some of which dated from the early part of the century.

Shortly before Bishop Svedberg was asked to prepare a hymnal to be used by the entire country, two minor publications were issued. They were the *Psalmeprover*, by Jacob Arrhenius, published in 1689, mostly with melodies, and a hymnal by Gabriel Magni Kling, published about 1690. The great hymnal of this period, however, was Svedberg's.

Svedberg's hymnal

In 1691, King Karl XI ordered Bishop Erik Benzelius to undertake the revision of the Swedish hymnal, with the help of Bishop Svedberg and Professor Israel Kolmodin. The royal instructions were that all hymns of impure teaching or otherwise unfit should be removed but that other existing hymns which were suitable, edifying, and spiritual should be retained. Haqvin Spegel, then bishop in Linköping, assisted considerably in the work and contributed about forty original, revised, or translated hymns. Jacob Arrhenius, professor of history at the University of Uppsala, also contributed some hymns. Bishop

---

[85] 30, p. 109.

Svedberg wrote sixteen hymns, translated twenty, and revised a great many.

The work was completed in 1693 and published the following year. It was immediately met with violent disapproval because of its unorthodox teachings. "Through its acceptance a new religion will be brought into our land" was the cry.[86] Consequently the entire output was confiscated although a number of copies were later sent to the Swedish colonists in America!

A committee was then appointed under Archbishop Sibelius to examine the hymnal. While most of the criticism was without foundation, about seventy hymns were omitted in the revised edition, several were modified, and six new hymns added. The new hymnal was published in 1695 and was called *Svedberg's* hymnal.

This edition contained no melodies. In 1697 it was re-issued with melodies and figured bass for organ, thus becoming the first Swedish hymnal with organ accompaniment. This became known as the *Koralpsalmboken,* and remained in use until the early nineteenth century.

The Koralpsalmboken

In the preparation of the musical counterpart of the hymnal, Svedberg suggested to the king that Olof Rudbeck and Harold Vallerius should get together with him and "let each hymn have its proper tune and notes."[87] While it is not unlikely that Rudbeck wrote some new melodies for the hymnal, the major part of the work was done by Vallerius, director of the Stockholm University music department.

According to Mankell,[88] the chorale book was made up of

---

[86] 13, p. 39.
[87] 23, Vol. II-III, p. 248.
[88] 23, Vol. I, p. 205.

material from (1) ancient Catholic songs and "Valdensare" (a religious sect) melodies, (2) folk tunes from the Middle Ages, (3) the stronger chorale style of Protestant melodies, (4) those borrowed from the Reformed Church and the Bohemian Brethren, (5) newer melodies of a lighter nature "with a lesser glowing power of faith."

Two excerpts from this work will be of interest.

Lof-va Gud,min själ, i   al - la stund Af hjer - tans grund!

Han föd - es   af en   - - - - jung - - fru   skär

The first fragment has a strong rhythmic pattern with a free use of syncopation. The second shows very prominently the influence of the Gregorian style imported from Germany.

The publication was generally well received although some criticized it for having too many melodies (262) of which a great number were never sung and could not be learned by the people in church. The *Koralpsalmboken* was also the signal for widespread use of the organ in accompanying congregational singing. "With the chorale book of 1697 with its general bass notation," says Norlind, "began the popular use of the organ as the accompanying instrument for congregational singing."[89] Vallerius employed notes of unequal rhythmic values, often used triple meter, which together with melodic embellishments gave the melodies more movement.

---

[89] 30, p. 116

The use of the organ

The early part of this period had experienced a great interest in choir singing. At the beginning of the seventeenth century the organ had been used to support the choir and to alternate with the choir in free instrumental parts as well as to intone the choral responses. The prominence of the organ, however, grew to the point where both the choir and congregation suffered from its misuse. Organists were cautioned not to perform "to gain fame for themselves" or to play music of questionable merit. They were instructed to "play slowly in intoning the psalms which the congregation sings."[90]

As in Germany, the chorale melodies in Sweden were subjected to decorative modifications including trills and mordents which destroyed their original character. The actual decline of the chorale in the Scandinavian countries lagged somewhat behind the movement in Germany. Pietism made its inroads into the northern countries as well, but the most devastating effects in church music came in the eighteenth and early nineteenth centuries when the conflict became acute between the foreign, unrhythmic (Gregorian) version of the chorale melodies and the rhythmic native religious folk music.

THE DANISH-NORWEGIAN CHORALE

Pontoppidan's hymnal

Denmark produced one publication in this period of particular importance: *Den Nye Psalme-Bog* by Eric Pontoppidan, published in 1740. Pontoppidan became bishop of Bergen, Norway, in 1748. While never authorized for use as a church hymnal, it was accepted by many.

The first edition of the hymnal consisted of a text edition

---

[90] 30, p. 115.

with a separate music section. In 1742 the hymnal was reissued with the melody for each hymn included with the text, as had been done in Thomissön's of 1569 and other publications.[91]

Pontoppidan's hymnal was patterned after Freylinghausen's *Gesangbuch* in Germany. Like Kingo, Pontoppidan made use of secular melodies, including dance tunes. The Norwegian historian, Sandvik, cites the following melody as representative of the type Freylinghausen introduced, some of which were borrowed by Pontoppidan.[92]

This is obviously not the type of melody one would associate with a hymn.

While Nicolai's melody *Wachet auf, ruft uns die Stimme* was given as follows in Babst's *Gesangbuch* of 1545.[93]

---

[91] Pontoppidan's was the last hymnal to have the melody and text together in the same book. After this, text editions and chorale books were issued separately.

[92] 34, p. 18. This melody is No. 133 in Pontoppidan's hymnal.

[93] From 38, p. 71. (The text for this title was not used in Babst's *Gesangbuch*.)

Pontoppidan has this version:[94]

Special mention should be made of the hymn writer Hans Adolph Brorson (1694-1764), whose hymns Pontoppidan generously included in his hymnal. Brorson represents the Pietistic group in direct opposition to Kingo. These opposing characteristics can best be illustrated by a selection from each.

O SEEK THE LORD TODAY

O seek the Lord today!
    Today He hath salvation;
Turn from thy sinful way
    In earnest supplication.
Repent and seek His grace,
    His call to thee doth sound;
O turn to Him thy face
    While yet He may be found.
        —H. A. Brorson,
        Trans. P. C. Paulsen

THE SUN ARISES NOW

The sun arises now
    In light and glory
And gilds the rugged brow
    Of mountains hoary;
Be glad, my soul, and lift
    Thy voice in singing
To God from earth below,
    Thy heart with joy aglow,
And praises ringing.
        —Thomas Kingo,
        Trans. P. C. Paulsen

---

[94] From 34, p. 163.

4

Reform and Devitalization

1750-1817

IN GERMANY

The eighteenth century was a period of secularization in both Germany and the Scandinavian countries. The dying days of Pietism gave birth to rationalism which reduced religion to the plane of ethics. Under Pietism the church had lost its interest in seriously promoting music. As a result music now went into the hands of secular composers almost to the exclusion of further development of the art within the church. The days of Palestrina and Bach were gone. This was the period of the opera under Handel and Gluck and the development of the orchestra under Stamitz. Through enlarged forms of orchestral composition, Haydn and Mozart were soon to explore further the potentialities of the orchestra as a medium of musical expression. The dynamic piano had replaced the feeble-voiced clavichord and the tawdry harpsichord as the chief keyboard instrument. The art of music had outgrown the narrow confines of the church but in addition to that, the church herself had pushed music out of its sanctum in no gentle manner. Theological trends influenced music.

Rationalism

Rationalism made its inroads into the hymns of the church through the subtle practice of revision. Some of the old hymns were in need of a revision to divest them of antiquated and uncouth expressions which had been carried with them from earlier periods. But the work of the rationalists went further than that. When their program of revision was over, there was little left for the devout worshiper. As it has been aptly expressed:

Instead of hymns of faith and salvation, the congregations were obliged to sing rhymed sermons on the existence of God, the immortality of the soul, the delights of reunion, the dignity of man, the duty of self improvement, the nurture of the body, and the care of animals and flowers.[95]

While texts thus suffered untold abuses and mutilations, the musical setting was not so extensively altered, the chief mark being the reduction of the rhythmic movement of the melodies to a movement of uniform note values.

With the revival of the evangelistic concept of theology in the early nineteenth century, the hymns were restored to their original meaning. It is because the rationalistic period contributed so little of lasting value that only a few hymns from this period are to be found in present hymnals. Most of the original hymns, with a few exceptions, were worse than the revisions.

Hymn writers

One of the finest poets of the time was Christian Gellert, professor of poetry and moral philosophy in Leipzig. He published his *Spiritual Odes and Hymns* in 1757. Gellert was a very gifted man and had not been carried far by the forces of rationalism.

---

[95] 115, p. 417.

Friedrich Klopstock, called the German Milton, published in 1758 a collection of original odes and included twenty-nine old hymns in altered form. His poetical style was fine but his hymns lacked popular simplicity. Other writers of the period include Johann Lavater and Matthias Claudius.

Musical settings

Hymn melodies, as has been mentioned above, were stripped of the Freylinghausen style of melodic ornamentation and reduced to a plodding movement of notes of equal duration. Very few original contributions of the period are to be found in current hymnals. One exception was Justin Knecht who wrote several numbers toward the end of the eighteenth century which are still in use.

The famous melody *Old Hundredth* by Louis Bourgeois from 1551 is a fine illustration of what happened to hymn melodies in this period. Bourgeois wrote the melody as follows:

We have come to know it only as a melody of equal note values with fermatas at phrase endings. Only recently have attempts been made by some composers to restore this melody to its original version.[96]

The following may be taken as being fairly representative of chorale settings for this period.[97]

---

[96] See No. 1 in the Presbyterian hymnal.
[97] 109, No. 139. Compare this with Freylinghausen's setting given on page 70.

In this work, the complete chords are written out instead of using only figured bass. This type of setting was now coming gradually into use.

The following example, which still used the figured bass, was published in 1817.[98]

[98] 42, page 83.

This example is the first listed in this series to have the upper staff written originally in the G clef. By this time, the notation of music had arrived at our present system. The Freylinghausen hymnal of 1741 is the first original work herein quoted to employ the bar line and meter signature in their modern usage. Chorale books published in the last quarter of the seventeenth century did not use bar lines to mark off measures.

Congregational singing of the type of music brought in by rationalism where note values tended to be of equal durational value, resulted in a dull, plodding movement which characterizes most chorale melodies yet today. It was during this period that the English historian, Charles Burney, traveled through Germany and other parts of Europe to learn firsthand of the state of music on the Continent. His observations are of great interest. His impressions received while attending high mass at the collegiate Church of St. Gudula in Brussels are recorded in these words:

I heard the performance of a considerable band of voices and instruments; and I was glad to find among the former two or three women, who, though they did not sing well, yet their being employed, proved that female voices might have admission in the church, without giving offence or scandal to piety, or even to bigotry. If the practice were to become general, of admitting women to sing the *soprano* part in the cathedrals, it would, in Italy, be a service to mankind, and in the rest of Europe render church-music infinitely more pleasing and perfect.[99]

[99] 10, Vol. I, p. 60.

Burney's surprise at finding women in the choir is accounted for by the fact that unchanged boys' voices customarily sang the soprano and alto parts. This is still done in Catholic, Anglican, and high Episcopal churches.

Of two Lutheran services attended in Germany, Burney had this to say:

I went this morning to the *Frauen Kirche,* or great Lutheran church of our Lady . . . The singing here, with so fine an instrument (organ), has a striking effect. The whole congregation, consisting of near 3,000 persons, sing in unison, melodies almost as slow as those used in our parish churches; but the people being better musicians here than with us, and accustomed from their infancy to sing the chief part of the service, were better in tune, and formed one of the grandest choruses I ever heard.[100]

. . .

I visited the *Thurmkirche* (Bremen) cathedral, belonging to the Lutherans, where I found the congregation singing a dismal melody, without the organ. When this was ended, the organist gave out a hymn tune, in the true dragging style of Sternhold and Hopkins. . . . The interludes between each line of the hymn were always the same, and of the following kind:

After hearing this tune, and these interludes repeated ten or twelve times, I went to see the town, and returning to the cathedral, two hours later, I still found them singing all in unison, and as loud as they could, the same tune, to the same accompaniment. I went to the post-office, to make dispositions for my departure; and, rather from curiosity than for the love of such music, I returned once more to this church,

[100] 10, Vol. II, pp. 30, 31.

and, to my great astonishment, still found them, vocally and organically performing the same ditty.[101]

This is a most remarkable commentary on the state of the chorale of about 175 years ago. While congregational singing today can often be justly criticized for its slow tempo, one must admit that a great deal of progress has been made since Burney visited the Bremen cathedral. To improve the tempo of chorales, the Brandenburg Synod fixed the length of the time unit in 1889 at one second as the slowest tempo to be used.

IN SWEDEN

Rationalism

Throughout the second half of the eighteenth century, Sweden was subjected also to the spirit of rationalism which was sweeping over the Continent. The tendency toward secularization was also strong and the church itself showed a "remarkable indifference for the musical part of the service."[102] Both the music and text degenerated. Hymn writers took advantage of their position in making the hymnal a battleground over dogmatic and aesthetic attitudes. *Den Svenska Provpsalmboken* of 1775-1777 is an illustration of this unfortunate period. Although the melodies taken from the 1697 chorale book were kept intact, they were often played with figurations and frills so that they retained little of the churchly spirit. Organ interludes between verses of the hymn became a favorite sport of the organists who otherwise found the chorale melodies slow and wearisome. The following example of *mellanspiel* (interludes) is cited as an illustration of this practice.[103]

---

[101] 10, Vol. II, pp. 279-281.
[102] 24, p. 440.
[103] 24, p. 443.

Hymn revisions

Under the rule of Gustaf III the influence of this "modernism" was so great that demands were made for a thorough revision of the hymnal. A proposed hymnal was published in 1793, the so-called Uppsala *Profsalmbok.* It was not found satisfactory with all positive Christian contents watered and filled with "grandiose empty phrases." In 1809 and again in 1811 Archbishop Lindblom appointed new committees to prepare hymnals but neither attempt met with success. The evangelical messages of the old hymns were changed and "in general they sought an empty display of words for the want of religious inspiration." For the greater part they were considered "dry didactic literary pieces; a pure and graceful language seemed to be the main thing and the contents lacked inherent pith and marrow."[104]

A number of minor hymn collections were published in Sweden in the eighteenth century. Some of these showed definite signs of foreign influence while others held to the official hymnody accepted by the Swedish Church. The tendency toward a rhythmical movement in their melodies was quite prominent and triple meter was becoming more frequent.

Chorale books

The first chorale book published in Sweden to have each of the four voices completely written out instead of melody with figured bass, was prepared by Georg Josef Vogler, director of music at the Stockholm opera, and published in 1798. While it was written out in a four-part setting, it was intended to be used as organ accompaniment to unison singing. It contained ninety musical settings of melodies from the 1697 chorale book for 260 hymns. It was not authorized for use by the church.

At the beginning of the nineteenth century, the matter of an adequate and up-to-date official chorale book became an item of great concern. A whole staff of musicians was selected to prepare it, including Vogler, Per Frigel, Åhlstrom, and J. C. F. Haeffner, who became a member of the committee in 1818. Frigel had already harmonized a great many chorales in vocal style and had retained the original rhythmic characteristics of the 1697 publication. Haeffner also prepared a four-voice chorale book in 1808 which also leaned toward the vocal style. He was Vogler's successor as director of the Stockholm opera, and was also known as court musician and as organist in the German church in Stockholm.

---

[104] These quotations are from 13, p. 44.

While both Haeffner and Vogler drew many of their melodies from a common source—the chorale book of 1697—the treatment given these melodies by the two men was quite different. Haeffner, who had close ties with the German group, introduced the type of setting which had come into use in Germany in which the melodies were largely reduced to notes of equal duration. This in itself was enough to provoke the anger of the Swedes as they had more than a mild preference for the more rhythmic type of melody akin to their folk music. To make matters worse, however, Haeffner also used the ancient Greek modes in harmonizing some of the melodies. Vogler, also a German, had promoted the 1697 chorale book style which the people had accepted as their own. He considered Haeffner too stiff and pedantic while Haeffner felt that Vogler was too free. Since Vogler had prepared his harmonizations as organ accompaniment to congregational singing, and since Haeffner had aimed to "vocalize" the chorale setting in such a way as to make it singable and at the same time adaptable for organ, this difference in the approach of the two men helped to widen the breach between them. "The two great Germans could no longer thrive together in Sweden," observes Nodermann,[105] so Vogler left the country giving Haeffner free rein to promote his ideas.

While Haeffner antagonized many with his treatment of the chorale, his "skill in harmonization," says Nodermann, "in spite of the opposition he experienced at that time has later won considerable acknowledgment as constantly rather rising than falling. On the other hand, his leveling-off principles [reducing the melody to notes of equal duration] and his German-ness even now cannot be forgotten and still today severe blows are directed

[105] 28, p. 50.

against his dead dust." Haeffner introduced a style which ever since has been a thorn in the flesh in Swedish chorale history.

The lack of rhythmic variety in Haeffner's melodies induced also slower singing. "The tempo of the melodies had already been retarded during the period when the choir accompanied congregational singing," comments Nodermann.[106] The tempo was further reduced when the choir was displaced by the organ which was found not only more convenient but also a great deal cheaper for the churches to maintain. However, in the large cathedrals the organ had to be played at a rather slow tempo. Thus the organ also contributed to the slow tempo used in chorale singing. Obviously Haeffner's music was not the kind which would offset the trend which was already under way.

But the great controversy over Haeffner did not develop until a few years later when he prepared a new chorale book which was adopted as the official publication by the church. This will be considered in a later section.

IN DENMARK AND NORWAY

The movement which was to oppose the secularization started by Kingo and continued by Pontoppidan was largely in the hands of men who, as in Sweden, were schooled in the German tradition and also did not meet with popular reception.

F. C. Breitendich

The first of these foreigners was F. C. Breitendich, organist at the royal court and at the St. Nicolai Church in Copenhagen. With the use of organs becoming more common in the eighteenth century, the old graduals of Jesperson and Kingo were found inadequate. A chorale book for the organist became a

---

[106] 28, p. 57.

necessity. The first such work for the Lutheran churches of Denmark and Norway was published by Breitendich in 1764. This was the *Fuldstaendig Koral-Bog* which contained old and new melodies with figured bass notation for hymnals then in use, particularly Pontoppidan's. In the preparation of this volume, Breitendich had drawn also on Jesperson's *Gradual* of 1573 and Freylinghausen's *Gesangbuch.* Some melodies were written down as he had heard them in his youth without any consideration of printed versions.

In his foreword, Breitendich says that the old melodies have been retained "as far as possible according to the Gradual and he has made no change other than time and custom have made and which, however, could not harm the melody."[107] For the new songs introduced, he followed Freylinghausen's hymnal and the Werningerode hymnal. The latter was in Freylinghausen's style and was widely used, having nine editions between 1712-1766.

Following is an example from Breitendich's chorale book as given by the Norwegian historian, Sandvik:[108]

---

[107] Quoted from 34, p. 19.

[108] The inner parts have been supplied. Breitendich wrote only the melody with figured bass added.

The following is a reproduction by Sandvik of page 17 of Breitendich's chorale book:

This will be recognized as Nicolai's *Wie schön leuchtet der Morgenstern.* Traces of the Freylinghausen practice of ornamentation are quite evident in these harmonizations.

Niels Schiorring

Another "reformer" in this period is found in Niels Schiorring. Schiorring had studied in Germany with C. P. E. Bach and was employed in the Royal Chapel. His chorale book was first published in 1781. In his preface he states that it is his purpose "to give our old church melodies their former simplicity and usefulness again as they were found at the time of Luther."[109] These

---

[109] Quoted from 34, p. 21.

he refers to as the "true church melodies, light and understand-
able without being flat or monotonous. They awaken the mind
to cheerfulness, joy, and devotion," Schiorring continues, "and
are not for play or pleasure as some of the newer ones by our
neighbors, the Germans." In Schiorring we find the reaction
against Pietism which characterized the music of the period in
Germany and Sweden. All the melodies are strictly regular in
time value with fermatas at every cadence. The following is an
example of a harmonized chorale as edited by Schiorring.[110]

H. C. O. Zinck

The third musical reformer in Danish-Norwegian hymnody
was H. C. O. Zinck, an immigrant German. He was commissioned to supply the needed melodies for *Evangelisk-Christlige
Psalme-bog,* published in 1798 by Balle.[111] Zinck was unaccus-
tomed to the Danish traditions and had no particular interest

---

[110] From 34, p. 22.

[111] Sandvik calls this hymnal the first main product of rationalism, and questions
whether it is either "evangelical" or "Christian" as the title indicates, and even if
it be a hymnal!

in the Danish language and thus was scarcely fit to edit a chorale book for his northern neighbors. Like Schiorring, Zinck had studied in Germany with C. P. E. Bach. His chorale book, published in 1801, was used extensively till the middle of the century.

Zinck's setting was in the traditional even-note rhythm characteristic of the German group in this period. The use of his music brought about a very low state of congregational singing. "With Zinck's chorale book," comments Sandvik, "the bottom was reached."[112] Organists, he states, being bored with the slow-moving music, would put in cadenza-like passages at the fermatas ending each line. As a further relaxation and opportunity for displaying their technique they would use "an operatic overture to usher people into church and a march or a waltz to usher them out again." Characteristic of the many criticisms against the type of congregational singing brought about by Zinck's chorale book is the following by C. G. Döderlein, director of the Asker Seminary, who wrote as follows:

Every member of the congregation sings the stated song as he had heard it sung in his childhood . . . according to the feelings the words in the song awaken in him. If therefore the spirit of the expression of the several stanzas is about the same, so that it *can* be recognized throughout the entire song, still the rhythm, the life and the movement by which these stanzas are sung, is endlessly different, as it must of necessity be where everything is so loose and free as here, where each one conducts himself as if he were the only one singing in the whole church. The songleader who should lead the singing of all, follows the same principles as does each one in the congregation and is distinguished chiefly by his lusty voice, which in the older, out-sung man becomes of necessity a shriek and a roar; and has he any difficulty in leading the song, it becomes for the most part an effort to drown out the other singers. If there

---

[112] 34, p. 24.

is an organ in the church, it goes its way also. Zinck's chorale book is used by the organist but he ornaments the melody with an endless number of trills, figurations, and interludes which often remind us of dances with which he regales us as the parish musician . . . he plays for his own enjoyment and fermatas become stopping places which stretch out by the minute. . ."[113]

Zinck's chorale book wrote the last chapter in the history of chorale decadence started by Pontoppidan when he issued his *Psalmebog* in 1740. The following versions of a phrase from Luther's *Ein feste Burg* show modifications made by various chorale book editors in Denmark:

a) *Thomissön*   b) *Kingo*

c) *Breitendich*   d) *Schiorring*

Thomissön's is most like the original version of Luther's song while Kingo's jumping rhythm retains little of the melody's characteristic stateliness. On the other hand, Breitendich and Schiorring divest it of all rhythmic variety.

With Schiorring, the harmony was more interesting than the melody. Both melodic and rhythmic changes were freely introduced by Schiorring in treating the old chorale melodies, as also the above excerpt shows. Schiorring's fermatas at the cadences are the signal for "a free little organ fantasia," says Sandvik[114] "which can be longer or shorter."

---

[113] Quoted from 34, pp. 35, 36.
[114] 34, p. 24.

The Breitendich-Schiorring-Zinck period in Denmark and Norway brought to these countries what Haeffner brought to Sweden. These men, however, cannot be held responsible for the technique they introduced. They were products of their time, trained in the technique of their period. This style seems to have met with a great deal more disfavor in the Scandinavian countries than it did in Germany. This may be because of two factors. First, they resented having these melodies imposed upon them by foreigners who still occupied the important musical positions in their churches and courts. Secondly, they had pre-served a lively interest in their native religious folk melodies which were distinctly rhythmic in character. They had no in-terest in the monotonous movement produced by the learned German musicians.

This period imposed upon Scandinavian chorales a mark which 150 years have not eradicated.

Revival

1817-1936

IN GERMANY

Reform from rationalism

Even though the first quarter of the nineteenth century saw a revival of the evangelical spirit of the Reformation, the ideas of rationalism still persisted throughout most of the century. This also influenced the hymnological and musical publications of the period. There existed a general feeling that church hymns and church music had lost their vitality the previous century and that there was great need for a general poetical and musical awakening.

One of the leaders of the revival movement in hymnology was Ernst Arndt, professor of history in Bonn. In 1819 his interest in the old hymns of the church resulted in a general revival which brought many of them back into use. Other poets, including Klopstock, Herder, Goethe, and Reichardt added their influence to the reform movement.

Among the writings of the period which strongly opposed the continued use of the hymns which came into use under rationalism, was Arndt's *The Word and the Church Hymn,* which pointed the way back to an evangelical interpretation of scriptural truths in the hymns. Rudolph Stier's *The Hymn-Book Misery* is another good example of the many writings which made their appearance on this subject.

The *Berliner Gesangbuch* of 1829 embodied notable reforms and set the example to be followed by many subsequent publications. By the 1860's most regions had received new hymnals, replacing those which had been issued under rationalism.

The nineteenth century was characterized not only by reform but also by research—the former being due to a great extent to the latter. Very profound hymnological studies were carried on throughout the century. This was a part of a more general pattern resulting from the surge of nationalism which followed the Napoleonic wars. A burning desire to learn more of the past and the origins of one's own culture was spreading and all phases of German history were being brought to the fore. So far as church music was concerned, the entire period from the Reformation on was brought under careful scrutiny. Peter Mortimer wrote on chorale singing in the time of the Reformation. Karl Winterfeld wrote extensively in several areas of church music and produced a three-volume history, the *Evangelische Kirchengesang* (1843-47), a significant research contribution of the period. Likewise, Philipp Wackernagel published a five-volume *Das deutsche Kirchenlied* in 1841.

Chorale books were also subjected to change as research showed that the more rhythmic forms of the early melodies had been reduced to a monotonous rhythmic movement under rationalism. Wilhelm Stahl lists twenty-four chorale books published between 1814-1866 which continued the rationalistic tendency.[115] Three are listed as being completely reformed,

---

[115] 36, pp. 113-117.

published between 1854-1888. Twenty others are given as containing partial reforms, published between 1844-1901.

The Eisenach chorale book

The Eisenach Conference in 1852 appointed a commission to "select 150 standard hymns, up to the middle of the eighteenth century, which were to form the common nucleus for the different territorial hymnbooks."[116] This collection was not intended only to reform the chorales, but also to supply a core of hymns which could be used in the Lutheran churches throughout Germany. Hitherto there had been no common hymnody. Each province or city issued its own hymnal. Thus there was the Nürnberg hymnal, the Marburg hymnal, the Stuttgart hymnal, the Halle hymnal, and so on, *ad infinitum*. The Eisenach Conference was an attempt on the part of the church governments to select a nucleus which could be in every hymnal. The full title of the so-called *Eisenach Choralbuch* was *Deutsches Evangelische Kirchen-Gesangbuch, in 150 Kernliedern*.

There is little reason to believe that this publication had any great influence in bringing about immediately a common hymnody. Its introduction at Lübeck met with partial success but other provinces reissued their own hymnals with their own melodies. Only the Bavarian hymnal of 1854 and the Hessian hymnal of 1888 fell completely in line with the Eisenach reform. The full impact of the Eisenach reform was not to be felt till in the early twentieth century.

Hymn writers

A number of outstanding hymn writers were active in the nineteenth century. One of the greatest writers was Karl J. P. Spitta, a Lutheran pastor and superintendent in Hannover. His

---

[116] 36, p. 116.

Psaltery and Harp passed through its fiftieth edition in 1884. Christian Barth of Stuttgart contributed a number of fine missionary hymns. Albert Knapp, also of Stuttgart, was a gifted writer. Only a few of his hymns have been translated into English. S. Preiswerk was one of the editors of the Basel *Gesangbuch* of 1854 and wrote several fine hymns.

Organ music also had its problems in this period. The decadent music of the early nineteenth century filled the immediate need of preludes and postludes, but because no contemporary music was appropriate for church use, organists fell to using the concert type of music written by Fogler, Mendelssohn, Rheinberger, and others. Some of these compositions became favorites although they were scarcely fitting for a church service.

The considerable interest in historical research in the earlier part of the nineteenth century continued on into the twentieth and brought forth the monumental six-volume study by Johannes Zahn, *Die Melodien der Deutschen Evangelischen Kirchenlieder* (1889-93), and the six-volume *Deutsche Evangelische Kirchenlied des 17. Jahrhunderts,* by Albert Fischer (1904-1916). Such an emphasis on research, however, came to be largely an end in itself and its direct value to the congregations at that time was meager. The re-editing of the old chorales in the light of research was a necessary move but neither the pastors nor the congregations were educated to the needs of the time. Pastors often took the view that church music was an ornament and was not indispensable. The congregation lacked a proper understanding of the place of music in the service because the use of school choirs in the church service had largely been discontinued. This has led, however, to a greater emphasis on *church* choirs—such as the Berlin Cathedral Choir—which aimed to bring noble music into the church. The growth of the church choir movement is an encouraging sign in German church music of the twentieth century. Through organizations such as the Church Choir Association, with over two thousand organizations affiliated, and the New Bach Society, significant contributions have been made toward a sympathetic understanding by all who are interested in church music.

Musical examples

A few musical examples from this period will be of interest.

(No meter signature given) 1826[117]

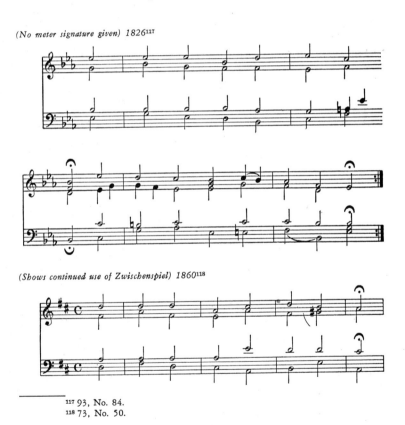

(Shows continued use of Zwischenspiel) 1860[118]

---

[117] 93, No. 84.
[118] 73, No. 50.

The opening and closing phrases of *Vom Himmel hoch* are given as follows in the Württemberg chorale book of 1876:[119]

---
[119] 45, page 10.

A more recent publication published in Berlin in 1911 gives in many cases both the rhythmic and nonrhythmic versions of the melodies. The following is given without meter signature:[120]

On the following page is given this version:

after which follows this note: "The original form of this chorale (see the foregoing number) let it be noticed, was set in this

---

[120] 82, No. 78.

melody; it is not, however, easy to perform. No wonder, that one therefore has set the melody in similar notes. Also in this form it possesses a special power and majesty, so that it—sung by a congregation—always produces a powerful impression."

Kulke gives three possible endings for *Vom Himmel hoch,* as follows:[121]

These illustrations show that a tendency toward a freer rhythmic movement in the chorale exists also in Germany. Kulke's chorale book demonstrates clearly the desire to get away from the stiff uniform movement introduced under rationalism.

The German publication which played an important role in church music in America was that of Dr. Friedrich Layriz, with the title: *Kern des deutschen Kirchengesangs.* According to his preface to this work, all the melodies are reproduced with their "original tone and rhythm" in so far as current means of reproducing them permitted. However, chorales dating from the period when "the crazy notion prevailed that a church song should be written only in notes of equal durational value" were subjected to a revision making them more varied. In regard to the harmonic setting, he says that he leans heavily on Johann Hermann Schein, although he has "permitted himself to use the dominant-seventh chord four times, three times allows a chromatic progression in the fundamental voice, and once in the tenor allows the interval of a diminished fifth."

He states that the use of the *Zwischenspiel* is less than one

---

[121] 82, No. 315.

hundred years old and suggests that it be used only at the end of each stanza, not at the endings of verse lines. The hymns are to be sung "in the tempo of a serious or cheerful folk song" and about fast enough that "every line can be comfortably sung in one breath." His book was first published in 1844.

Following is Layriz's setting of Luther's *Ein feste Burg*:[122]

The C clef is employed throughout the book for the upper staff. The misplacement of some of the notes in the second and fourth measures found in the original has been retained here. Layriz maintains rhythmic variety throughout the two-hundred settings in his work, twenty-two of which are in triple meter.

A second edition of his book came out in two volumes in 1849. The first volume contains 130 of the most appropriate chorales for church use and the second volume contains 200 for choir and family use, with a supplement of 17 additional selections, the G clef having been substituted for the C clef throughout.

In his preface to the second edition he states that "pains were taken to preserve conformity with the sources," and claims to be the first to introduce six-four meter.

---

[122] 84, No. 42.

A third edition of four volumes (the fourth being entirely liturgical music) containing 613 hymn settings came out over a period of years shortly after the middle of the century. It is interesting to note that while Layriz repeatedly states that the chorales are put in their original rhythmic version and that he has followed closely the sources, he has different versions of many melodies in each of these three editions. Hassler's melody to which *O Sacred Head Now Wounded* is sung is given as follows in the first edition:[123]

while in the second edition it appears as follows:[124]

The first edition has this version of *O Christe Morgensterne*:[125]

The second edition has this version:

The third edition has this version:[126]

[123] 84, No. 84.
[124] 84, Vol. I No. 52.
[125] 84, No. 144, Vol. II No. 275, and Vol. II No. 273 respectively.
[126] Meter signatures are seldom given in the third edition.

Were the writer of this book to edit this melody, he would likely give it this version:

because the third measure of Layriz's versions in the second and third editions are not in six-four meter but in three-two.

The unification of the chorales in Germany is continuing. In the wake of the Eisenach reforms the early twentieth century produced the *General Evangelical Hymn Book* of 1906-10, the *Deutsches Auslands* hymnal of 1915, and the *Deutsches Evangelisches Gesangbuch* of 1926 with its accompanying *Melodienbuch* issued the following year. The *Melodienbuch,* containing the musical settings, represents a return to the more rhythmic type of chorale melody which had been introduced by the Eisenach chorale book. There is considerable doubt as to the advisability of this practice, however, since the use of polymetric forms thereby necessitated is very difficult to impose upon congregations with tradition two centuries old of singing in the even movement of isometric melodies.

A number of problems have made complete unification exceedingly difficult. Many areas have been opposed to reforms as such. A great number of "spiritual songs," largely of the folk song type, and "evangelical" and "kingdom" songs (witness the popularity of Spitta's *Psaltery and Harp*) have found their way into hymn publications. There has also been a greater emphasis on research than on the creative writing of hymns. In spite of difficulties, however, progress has been made. Demands for uniform hymnals have been repeated again and again. No longer is the uniformity of a number of texts and melodies felt adequate, but the uniformity of complete hymnals is demanded. The Berlin hymnals of 1906 and 1910 which embodied these ideals, however, were rejected. The compilers of the Frankfort hymnal of 1927 attempted further unification by including 342 hymns from the 1926 *Evangelisches Gesangbuch* for its first part and then added a second part containing their own treasury of hymns. A hopeful sign that unification will continue is found in the fact that hymnals are no longer compiled by individuals but by the church itself through its regular channels of publication.

IN SWEDEN

The reform movement in Sweden started somewhat later than in Germany. While Svedberg's hymnal had continued in popular use up to this period, the time was now ripe for a revision of the entire Swedish hymnological material. This resulted in what is known as Wallin's hymnal, which, subjected to numerous revisions and additions, has remained in use till the present time.

Wallin's hymnal

In 1811, the king appointed a special committee to prepare a new hymnal to take the place of Svedberg's which had served well for over a century. The committee released its *Förslag till forbattrade Kyrko-Sanger* in 1814. The proposed hymnal contained 413 hymns. It did not meet with popular approval. The task of carrying on the work was then turned over to Johann Olof Wallin, who had been a member of the hymnal committee. Wallin had previously won recognition for his poetical gifts while attending the University of Uppsala and was well prepared for the task. He completed his work in 1819 at which time his hymnal was authorized for use by King Karl XIV.

Wallin's hymnal contained 500 hymns, of which 128 were his own, 178 were revisions by him, 23 were his translations and 13 were semioriginal, based on hymns by others. Other poets who contributed included Franzén, Nyström, Geiger, Afzelius, Hedborn, and Åström.

A revised edition of Wallin's hymnal was prepared by J. H. Thomander and P. Wieselgren and published in Malmö in 1849. Several hymns were altered to conform with modern interpretations of Scripture. In 1920, an appendix of 173 hymns was added, containing contributions by more contemporary writers, such as Lina Sandell, Rosenius, Johann Eklund, Svante Alin, Edvard Evers, Eric Södeberg, and some by hymn writers of the Reformed churches.

Haeffner's chorale book of 1820-1821

From the musical standpoint, the struggle between the native rhythmic chorale and the stiff, nonrhythmic chorale introduced by Haeffner continued at a bitter pace. An enlarged and revised edition of Haeffner's work was published in two parts, Part I in Stockholm in 1820 and Part II in Uppsala the following year. The new publication introduced also a number of new melodies with not less than ninety taken mainly from two German publications prepared by König and Kühnau. König's chorale book had served as a model for Haeffner in preparing his own.

Introducing more foreign melodies added fuel to the fire created by Haeffner's chorale book of 1808. The people had become accustomed to the old hymns which their fathers and mothers had sung and would have nothing to do with these new melodies. In some instances feeling ran so high that parents compelled their children to swear by the Bible that they would not sing them. The organists would "let these chorale songs roar forth with all the strength which organ performance was capable of; they became a hostile power, directed against the congregation's old and, for her, cherished cultural inheritance."[127] This resulted in a strife between the organists and congregations throughout the nineteenth century. Moberg states that "what happened during the nineteenth century has caused great harm to church song and also to Swedish musical culture."

The period of uncertainty regarding the musical setting of the chorale caused by the continued use of Vallerius' outdated *Koralpsalmboken* and the failure of the government to authorize a more modern version was brought to an end by Haeffner but his work was given a hostile reception by musicians and laity alike.

Frigel, who was secretary of the Music Academy and member of the hymn committee till 1818—the time when Haeffner came in—had engaged in a number of duels with Haeffner in various newspapers and magazines regarding the latter's theories for the musical setting. Comments like these came from Frigel's pen as he criticized Haeffner's chorales: "Certainly not a masterpiece . . . delightful bass . . . what a modulation!. . . trivial and monotonous . . . what a torture to one's ear!. . . a great absurdity."[128]

In spite of such criticisms, the musically qualified members of the hymnal committee which examined Wallin's hymnal passed judgment on Haeffner's music as well and found it the best available for the hymns included. Mankell states that these "musically qualified" members were Stolpe, rector in Stockholm, who had no intimate knowledge of music; E. G. von Rosén, a talented organist but without formal instruction in music; Åhlström, also an organist but poorly qualified musically, and

[127] 24, p. 463.
[128] 23, Vol. II-III, p. 288.

Frigel, whom Mankell calls the only member who could intelligently express himself on Haeffner's chorales.

An examination of Volume I of Haeffner's chorale book reveals that fifty-one per cent of his harmonizations are in minor keys, including his use of the old modes of minor feeling. His use of the old modes is rather extensive. No. 158, in the Mixolydian mode has this ending:

Almost all chorales are in two-two or four-two meters, although C is often used to designate both. Six chorales are given double meter signatures: three-two C or three-two ¢. Such mixed meters appear to be used in order to set the old melodies in modern notation without extensive alterations.

To illustrate how older melodies were reduced to notes of equal duration, compare the first melody on page 78, taken from the 1697 *Koralpsalmboken* with Haeffner's version (No. 390).

In some localities Haeffner's chorale book was accepted because it was considered as good as any available. "It may surely stand with honor beside most foreign publications," writes Mankell.[129] He adds, however, "It cannot be denied that Haeffner overlooked or pretended not to know a number of German chorale treasures which were well worth being taken up even in the Swedish chorale book." Moberg concludes, "We believe that one shall gradually understand that the best, the vital and important in the criticisms of Haeffner's chorale book on the whole gained consideration, and the objections one might have against the new chorale book are on a different level."[130]

From this time on to the present Swedish chorale book editors have tried to bring the spirit of the 1697 chorale book into their chorale versions. While many of the subsequent chorale books have been largely revisions of Haeffner's, a gradual move away from the Haeffner style has been noticed.

Continued reform

In 1832, a chorale book was issued by Olof Åhlström, in which he attempted to maintain a middle course in the controversy between the rhythmic and nonrhythmic chorales. He subjected the chorales to a thorough revision in an attempt to bring them back to their original Swedish style. His work was well received, but a number of the melodies were in too high a register for congregational singing.

In 1858, what came to be known as *Petterssons Koralpsalmbok* was published. This was the first *Koralpsalmbok,* i.e. having both the text and full musical setting, to be published since 1697. This was also opposed to Haeffner, with a number of melodies in the old rhythmic form. This publication was widely

---

[129] 23, Vol. II-III, p. 283.
[130] 24, p. 541.

used, having its fourth edition in 1875 and its tenth in 1901.

Meanwhile the Haeffner type of chorale was bringing about a pitiable state of congregational singing. The melodies were dragged out at an exceedingly slow tempo and the hymns with from twenty to thirty stanzas seemed without end. To help solve this problem a booklet was prepared by P. A. Heischman in which he suggested that "three seconds be allotted for each note in chorales of joy and celebration; four seconds for those of sad and grave character, with the cadence tones held somewhat longer and the pauses after the cadences to be from two to four seconds respectively."[131] Considering "America" as a song of "grave character," it would take about nine minutes to sing three stanzas according to the suggested tempo, whereas we sing it in about one and one-half minutes! And Heischman's suggestion was recommended to *improve* the singing!

The struggle between the Haeffner type and the native rhythmic type of chorale melody, however, continued with the pastors apparently taking more interest than the organists. In 1860, C. J. Lewerth published what was essentially an edition of Haeffner's chorale book although some changes were made in both the melodies and the harmonic setting.

In 1864, Abraham Mankell published a *Koralpsalmbok*. While Mankell was an avowed opponent of Haeffner, Nodermann criticized him for evening out the note values even more than did Haeffner. Both the Mankell and Pettersson publications, however, made rather free use of triple meter, whereas this is scarcely found in Haeffner.

Another revised Haeffner book was published in 1877 by J. A. Josephson. This work had been started by Frank Berwald but upon his death in 1868 was continued by Josephson. While

---

[131] 24, p. 462.

the publication is definitely "Haeffnerian," it is considered a great improvement.

A chorale book opposed to the Haeffnerian style was published by Israel Sandström, also in 1877. Sandström employed a more rhythmic version of the melodies, using a Norwegian publication by Ludwig Lindeman as model. He included also a number of melodies not found in Haeffner.

The first genuine threat to the Haeffner style came with the publication of C. E. Södling's *Svensk Folkets Choralmelodier* in 1878. But four years later another Haeffner edition was released by B. V. Hallberg in which a number of the less-used Haeffner melodies were omitted and an appendix of new melodies added, drawn mostly from the Württemberg chorale book of 1844. Several additional publications came out toward the end of the century, such as Törnwall's in 1882, Hultstedt's in 1885, Heintze's in 1889, Rendal's in the same year, Lindström's *Koralpsalmbok* in 1892, and Anjou's chorale book in 1899— all belonging to the Haeffner camp. Those who advocated the more rhythmic type included publications by Humbla in 1885, Lagergren in 1886, Ullman in 1890, and Stockenberg in 1899.

In 1903, the *Svensk Koralbok* (*efter Haeffner*) was published by Nordqvist and Lagergren, essentially a revision of Haeffner's work, though more flexible in rhythmic treatment.

Examples of the melody to which the Swedish hymn *Ach, hjertans ve* was sung in some of these publications follow.

Haeffner, No. 98

Mankell, No. 55

Nordqvist-Lagergren, No. 98a

Lindström, No. 98

Lundblad, No. 3

What a Tower of Babel this was! No wonder congregational singing has had its difficulties with so many versions of a single melody appearing in a couple generations' time!

Nordqvist and Lagergren suggested that the tempo for songs of praise should be to sing a quarter-note at 60 M.M. (one note per second), while selections such as Luther's *Ein feste Burg* be taken somewhat slower. Passion hymns, communion hymns, funeral songs, and so on, should be taken still slower.

While Lindström seems to prefer a rhythmic pattern less rigid than Haeffner, he allies himself definitely with the non-rhythmic group. In his preface he states "In regard to the chorales from the new hymnal, Wallin was from the beginning doubtful whether he should adhere to the more conservative

Haeffner or to the more modern Frigel-Åhlström faction. Thanks to Geiger's influence, he allied himself with Haeffner, whose great merit it was that the Swedish chorale book has such a rich resource in charming and worthy melodies."

The Friends of Church Song

In 1876, Bishop U. L. Ullman in his *Evangelisk-Luthersk Liturgik states* that there is a need for a "congregational song of a livelier disposition, of more life and power than the drawn-out, drowsy melodies which one ... nevertheless not seldom gets to hear in our regular church services."[132] In 1889 a group of pastors, among them G. T. Lundblad (1851-1931), formed a male quartet to sing church music and arouse an interest in what they saw needed to be done to improve the deplorable situation resulting from the years of strife precipitated by Haeffner. Two years later they had a following large enough to form an organization "for the improvement of the church song within the congregations of the bishopric."[133] Bishop U. L. Ullman (d. 1930), Rikard Norén (d. 1922), and J. T. Morén (d. 1932) became leaders of the new movement. Bishop Ullman was a member of the hymnal committee delegated in 1889 to revise Wallin's work, and in 1890 prepared an edition of Elfrida Andrée's chorales as a temporary expedient until a new chorale book could be prepared. In his preface to this work he states how he aimed to set the chorales in their "original form," so that the congregations could sing the hymns "as their fathers did." He reminds his people of the 1697 chorale book as being of peculiarly Nordic character and genuineness "of which Haeffner in his chorale book almost entirely deprived us."[134]

---

[132] Quoted from 24, p. 468, 469.
[133] 24, p. 499.
[134] 24, p. 500.

Norén and Morén collaborated in the preparation of their *Valda koraler i gammalrytmisk form* (Selected Chorales in the Old Rhythmic Form), in which their rhythmic system was based on the theories of the ancient Greek philosopher, Aristoxenos! They criticized the German writers such as Layriz for their treatment of the rhythmic structure.

The Friends of Church Song took their matter seriously. Bishop Ullman who gave the opening address at the first meeting of the association in Linköping in May, 1898, stated ". . . it is a question about nothing less than a great church matter of eminent importance for our people, especially for our youths' religious welfare, edification, and ennoblement, yes, its churchly nourishment."[135] The association published through its secretary, G. T. Lundblad, *Svensk Koralbok i reviderad rythmisk form* (Swedish Chorale Book in Revised Rhythmic Form) in 1901. This was followed by an improved edition the following year. From the foreword to the first edition of Lundblad's book, we quote: "One begins more and more to understand that something needs to be done to free our hymn melodies from their century-old shackles and assist them to a new rhythmical and naturally lively beauty...." He made free use of three-two, six-four, and three-four meters and also double signatures of three-two and six-four.

While the Lundblad book is distinctly opposed to the stiff Haeffnerian movement, Nodermann comments that "It is possible to play several high masses from this book without the congregation knowing other than that the organist played from Haeffner's chorale book."[136]

Johann Lindegren (d. 1908) published a work in 1905 in

[135] 21, p. 7.
[136] 28, p. 93.

which he presented the melodies in both the old and new rhythmic versions. While he favored rich harmonization and a good movement in the chorale, at the same time he tried to retain as much as possible of the older practice. Some of Haeffner's melodies are retained unaltered. In his preface he states that "To render the important melodies from the Protestant Chorale's golden age—the sixteenth and seventeenth centuries—readily accessible in their most genuine form, so that friends of churchly art with ease can place themselves in this music genus and also that interest for its practical use be entirely common is the aim of this work."[137]

The Nodermann-Wulff chorale book of 1911 retains rather strong Haeffner characteristics although it introduced freer rhythmic movement without aiming to return to "old rhythmic" patterns as was characteristic of the Friends of Church Song movement. The Nodermann-Wulff work, therefore, represents a reaction against the Friends of Church Song movement because it identifies itself with the Haeffner style.

Further evidence of a reaction against the Friends of Church Song is seen in a publication by Hugo Bedinger, organist at Våsterås, who published in 1911 his chorale book "with hymn melodies as they correctly should be set forth."[138] He opposed the Friends of Church Song practice in their use of three-two, six-four, and five-four meters and sought "to give the 'natural rhythm'" in closer agreement with Haeffner's work, "whose chorale book," Bedinger states "was lightly judged and sentenced by so many."

After having been subjected to the two extremes of Haeffner and the Friends of Church Song, Sweden has just in the last few

---

[137] 28, p. 93.
[138] 24, p. 506.

decades arrived at a rather satisfactory solution to her problem. In 1916 an official chorale book committee was formed and commissioned to prepare a new chorale book for the church. Members of this committee included Otto Olsson from the Stockholm Conservatory. Their work was published in 1921. A number of melodies were taken from Haeffner and the chorale book of 1679 with the melodies from the latter source in a simplified rhythmic form. A number of Haeffner's chorales were excluded. Compositions by contemporary Swedish composers were included, among them four by Johann Lindegren, one each by Morén and Norén, and three by Otto Olsson.

Many Swedish church musicians conceive the new chorale book of 1921 as a defeat for the search for the rhythmic chorale which above all characterized the Friends of Church Song—and so no doubt it is.

A supplementary collection of a group of proposed alternative chorales was published in 1934. This publication lists thirty-four melodies of the 1921 publication as unsuited. Thirty-three melodies in the supplement are by recent composers, notably Gunnar Wennerberg.

A school publication of this period, *Folkskolans Koral-Psalmbok* by N. E. Anjou, published in Stockholm in 1922, shows also the very definite trend toward the more rhythmic type of hymn melody. While an edition of *Den Swenska Psalmboken* published in Oerebro in 1823 has this melody:

No. 298

Anjou's book has this version of the same melody:

121

IN NORWAY

Independence

During the period of the Napoleonic wars, Norway was completely cut off from Denmark. This resulted in a heightened spirit of nationalism among the Norwegians. At the close of the war, the great powers, England, Prussia, Russia, and Austria, were determined that Norway should not remain under Danish rule but be given to Sweden. This was done when the peace was written in 1814. Sweden, however, recognized a constitution drawn up by the Norwegians so that Norway was given virtually an autonomous government. This arrangement existed until 1905 when Norway gained complete independence.

As long as Norway was a part of Denmark, Copenhagen with its university, large churches, the royal palace, and other spheres of influence remained the one great cultural center for both countries. Norway did not develop as favorably in the fields of art and music as did Denmark. The growth of a distinctly Norwegian music and literature did not begin till the early nineteenth century. During the second half of the century, the first far-reaching attempts were made to produce a Norwegian hymnody based on purely Norwegian traditions. Several factors now made this possible. The first, naturally, was the separation from Denmark and the forming of what was practically an autonomous government, linked loosely with Sweden. The second factor was that the first generation of German-trained musicians had passed, and while Norwegian musicians still went to the Continent or to Denmark to study, there was a greater urge to develop a nationalistic type of music and not merely to imitate the foreigners. A third factor to be considered is that through centuries of rather erratic development, Norway had gleaned some church music which could be rightly called her own. This does not mean that the originally Danish hymns which had been used in Norway were now to be discarded. On the contrary, the better-liked Danish hymns together with the Norwegian hymns formed the nucleus around which the new hymnody was to develop.

Ole Andreas Lindeman

Coming of age as a nation meant also supplying music for the church which would be more indigenous to their worship. Zinck's chorale book had been used but now a change was in order.

The leader in music at the moment was O. A. Lindeman, organist in *Vor Frue Kirke* in Trondhjem, a position he had occupied since 1799. Lindeman had studied in Copenhagen and had returned to Norway at the age of twenty-four. He was asked to prepare a chorale book to serve as a common melody book for Kingo's, Guldberg's, and Balle's hymnals and thus promote uniformity in church song. Lindeman was instructed to give the entire chorale literature a critical revision and to restore the chorales as far as possible to their original character. His chorale book was published in 1838 and was accepted as the replacement of Zinck's and other collections which had remained in use.

From his introduction to this work we learn that Lindeman felt it necessary to give the chorales a critical examination because of the many differences which existed in the Breitendich,

Schiorring, and Zinck chorale books. He complains that not only do certain notes differ but entire phases. He comments that the practice of adapting the melodies written in the old ecclesiastical modes to the modern major and minor scales has resulted in the destruction of their original character. He attempted, he says,

on the one hand to avoid monotonous harmony which becomes boring and tiring for the ear, and on the other to avoid unnecessary passing tones, chromatic and enharmonic progressions whereby the harmony in place of enhancing the melody renders it unrecognizable by concealing it under a bombast of successive dissonances. . . While the harmony which is found in the chorale book is not the only possible version, it is understood that the organist is not bound to use this version but that he may alter the harmonization for each stanza. . .[139]

This last sentence implies that his book is written for organ, although "its use for four singing voices is not thereby rejected or made impossible," he continues, although he feels that the choir should sing in unison with the congregation.

As compared with his predecessors, Lindeman used a more modern harmonic idiom and instead of using the conventional repeat sign for repeated periods, he gave the repeated melodic unit a new harmonization. While these are notable improvements, the book also had its shortcomings. The rhythmic pattern is definitely of the Haeffner type—pages and pages of half notes, interrupted only occasionally by a quarter note. All but five of the 186 chorale settings are in two-two meter. Some melodies, such as his No. 8, *Al den ganske Christenhed,* which was in triple meter in earlier collections is now set in duple meter with notes of equal duration. He was as opposed to the three-beat measure as was Zinck.

---

[139] 87, Introduction.

The following example:

had this version in the Erfurt Enchiridion of 1524 which
Thomissön had retained with only slight change.[140]

Lindeman's version of *Ein feste Burg* is a series of half notes
all the way through. The opening period follows:

The authorization of O. A. Lindeman's chorale book brought
about a "song-strife" similar to that in Sweden. While Zinck's
work was generally blamed for the difficulty in hymn singing,
Lindeman's book didn't improve matters and since it was authorized for exclusive use in the churches, it received much of the
blame.

Some felt that the low state of congregational singing was

---

[140] Taken from 34, p. 108.

the fault of the organ. The congregation "cannot distinguish the individual tones in a harmony and grasp the melody"[141] was the complaint of some. One writer found that "the organist plays according to O. A. Lindeman, but the greater part of the congregation sings according to the old melodies."[142] His melodies are criticized as "cold and stiff." There is a demand on the part of some for the rhythmic version. G. Bergh, a seminary teacher, found that half of Lindeman's melodies were not usable because they lacked melody and therefore were too difficult. His harmonization is criticized as a "seeking after musical effect"—the harmony has become the important thing and robs the melody of its beauty. Some argued that the congregation is entitled to sing the old version of the melodies and that the church song in general should as far as possible be similar to the old folk song type of melody.

There is also the question whether the melodies ought not be in their original form as the composer wrote them and congregations sang them "until the last century's desire to change, lacking in taste and churchly sense or depth, particularly to remove their rhythmic features, handling them in such a manner as to render most of them unrecognizable . . ."[143]

Others did not place the blame for poor congregational singing on Lindeman's chorale book, but felt it was because the chorales were sung in such a slow tempo in rehearsals at the seminary. But the seminaries have their own complaints about the differences in practice in the various churches. Döderlin of the Asker Seminary states that,

To begin with, the music teacher at the seminary must be acquainted with all congregations in the diocese and he must also be a man who

---

[141] 34, p. 30.
[142] 34, p. 40.
[143] 34, p. 34.

can appropriate and write down each congregation's version [of each melody] and he must be certain for which congregation each student is preparing so that he can get the proper version and he must finally also be certain that the student remains in the congregation and that this version should not be strange to the congregation should he move to another place or it would be necessary to teach each student all versions, and this must be recognized as being impossible. . . .[144]

O. A. Lindeman's chorale book created a stir similar to Haeffner's in Sweden. Such was the reception given the first Norwegian chorale book!

Hymnals

By the middle of the nineteenth century, a number of more popular hymn books were available. Among them were books by the Danish hymn writers, Grundtvig (*Sang-Värk til den Danske Kirke,* 1837), and Guldberg, and a hymnal by the Norwegian lay-preacher, Hans Nielsen Hauge. Kingo's hymnal was revised under the supervision of B. S. Ingemann and re-issued in 1855.

It remained for a Norwegian minister in Telemark, M. B. Landstad, to bring order out of the heterogeneous hymnody which had developed and to produce a Norwegian hymnal more to the wishes of the people. Landstad was well qualified to take over this difficult task. He had won renown as a writer of religious poetry and his keen interest in Norwegian folk music had netted him a sizable collection of religious folk songs gathered mainly from the Telemark area.

Landstad prepared his hymnal with the skill of an artisan. Fifty of his own hymns were included. When it was published in 1869 it was authorized for use by a resolution by the king. This has since been the most generally used hymnal in Norway.

---

[144] 34, p. 37.

Ludwig M. Lindeman

The man who was to collaborate with Landstad in supplying Norway its first satisfactory congregational hymnal was Ludwig M. Lindeman, organist at *Vor Frelsers Kirke* in Christiania (now Oslo), and son of Ole Andreas Lindeman. Ludwig Lindeman and Landstad had previously prepared an edition of Luther's *Geistliche Lieder* in 1859 under the title of *Martin Luthers Aandelige Sange*. They had carefully preserved the original rhythmic characteristics of the melodies, although syncopation was removed. To these melodies, Lindeman added a setting for four voices.

With the publication of Landstad's *Psalmebog* in 1869, Ludwig Lindeman undertook the task of preparing a new chorale book. This undertaking he completed in 1871, issuing the book in two parts. The first part contained the melodies not found in his father's book and the second part contained melodies from his father's book. He sought to rectify the evils of his father's and Zinck's chorale books. In his foreword he states he has omitted "all that can be a hindrance for good church song."

Fifty-four of his own chorales are included in the publication. A number of these have met with popular favor.[145] He suggested that the quarter note be substituted for the half note in the interest of reducing printing costs, thus breaking with the hitherto common practice of using the half note as the beat unit. The use of irregular rhythm was removed, substituting ♩ ♩ ♩ ♩ ♩ ♩, for though there are some devices of this type to be found in his own chorales. A partial restoration of a more rhythmic pattern was effected by the rather frequent use of ♩. ♪ instead of ♩ ♩, although the regular quarter note pattern is followed

---

[145] His "Built on the Rock" has become a universal favorite.

extensively. Instead of fermatas at the endings, the ending note is frequently an eighth note followed by an eighth rest. In his preface he suggests that the tempo be $\quarternote = 60$ M.M. or a little less, according to the circumstances. He states also that those organists who are adequately trained may use their own harmonizations—differing for each stanza, but warns that those who are not sufficiently trained in harmony and performance should play exactly as written.

Copies of Lindeman's book were sent to all pastors in the country and in many places it was put into immediate use. It was well received—7,000 copies were sold in six years. Lindeman's work represents a blending of the old with the newer trends in chorale music, preparing the way for still further progress. The rhythmic movement he gave the melodies ended the period of song-strife which existed as long as his father's book was used.

A comparison of how Nicolai's *Wie schön leuchtet der Morgenstern* is handled by O. A. Lindeman and his son, Ludwig, will show the main characteristics of the differences in style.

O. A. Lindeman, No. 4

Ludwig Lindeman, No. 2

Eric Hoff

An unauthorized chorale book was published in 1878 by Eric Hoff, for organ, piano, or mixed choir. It contained settings for the Hauge, Landstad, *Evangelisk-Kristelige,* Guldberg, and

Kingo hymnals, as well as the hymnal for the Norwegian Evangelical Lutheran Church in America. This publication is mentioned here only because of the problem of the rhythmical version of the chorale. In his preface, Hoff states that,

Throughout the Lutheran church especially in the last fifty years, there has been expressed the wish that congregational singing be improved. One felt that it had gone to pieces, and that those who understood and had something to do with it, talked loudly and still talk about the chorale's condition, but they are incompetent and unsatisfactory.

Commenting on the contest between the rhythmic and non-rhythmic chorale versions, he states

. . . the correct way is to let the melodies retain their original rhythmic form so far as they can be used by the congregation. Let both the rhythmic and nonrhythmic forms work side by side.

In carrying out this plan, Hoff frequently gives two versions of the melody, as:

No. 151

which is also given in what he calls "chorale form":

Revisions of both Landstad's hymnal and Lindeman's chorale book were made in the first quarter of the twentieth century. Gustav Jensen's revision of the hymnal in 1915 introduced a number of hymns for which there were no melodies in Lindeman's chorale book and some of the old melodies had no texts in the new hymnal. An appendix of new melodies was considered but this was discarded in favor of preparing a new chorale book, the *Koralbok for den Norske Kirke*, published in 1926. Religious folk tunes of Norway contributed most of the new melodies in this collection. A few of Ludwig Lindeman's settings were omitted and those retained subjected to minor modifications. A number of originally composed musical settings are also included. A revised edition was published in 1936 in which a number of chorales were transposed into a lower key. The selection of melodies was made to provide for the hymnals then in use, the *Gamle Landstad, Landstad's Reviderte Kirkesalmebog, Nynorsk Salmebok,* and *Hauge's Salmebog.*

IN DENMARK

Reorganization

The close of the Napoleonic war in 1814, resulting in the loss of Norway, was followed in Denmark by a period of political and social agitation and reorganization. This period brought forth the adoption of a liberal constitution in 1849. From the viewpoint of church organization, the country was almost entirely Lutheran.

Bishop Grundtvig

Bishop Grundtvig is easily the greatest hymn writer of the period. His *Sang-Värk til den Danske Kirke* was published in 1837 with subsequent editions following throughout the century. His *Festsalmer* was published in 1850.

Another important publication was the *Roskilde Konvents-Salmebog* published in 1855. Its chief feature was the restoration of the old hymns to their original form. These hymns had been rewritten or in some cases almost wholly destroyed in the earlier *Evangelisk-kristelige Salmebog* by Balle, issued in the rationalistic period. Another hymnal was published by a clerical synod at Roskilde in 1873, the *Salmebog til Kirke- og Hus-Andagt.*

Danish and German music parted early in the nineteenth century, largely due to Grundtvig's influence. The old stiff chorale melodies were not suitable for Grundtvig's texts. In order to supply melodies for the new hymns, the Danes did as the Pietists had done: went to secular sources or dressed up older church melodies in their likeness. The form, technique and method of the Romantic composers were employed in supplying melodies for the new hymns.

The following is an illustration of the type of melody employed.[146]

Chorale publications

Like Sweden and Norway, Denmark also fought the non-rhythmic version of the chorale melodies. Chorale books by Weyse in 1839 and Berggreen in 1853 continued in the stiff style introduced under rationalism, but Rung's of 1857 and Barnekow's of 1892 represent the newer trend. The Danish historian, Thuner, comments that,[147]

As an attempt to revive the rhythmic congregational song of the period of the Reformation on a Danish basis similar to endeavors which are

---

[146] 79, No. 14.
[147] 120, p. 17.

made in Germany, Thomas Laub issued in 1888-90 and again in 1896-1909 hymn melodies in church style, which in 1918 was followed by a complete collection of Danish church song (supplements in 1925-1930), and which in addition to old melodies in rhythmical form contains a great number of melodies by himself.

Laub's first work, his *Kirkenmelodier* (1888-90) consists of three volumes, making it a very complete collection of hymn melodies. Like his Scandinavian brethren, Laub sought to restore the more rhythmic version of the chorales.

In 1901, *Melodier til Psalmebog for Kirke og Hjem* was published by V. Bielefeldt. This has been widely used. It was in its fifteenth printing in 1943. This publication represents prominently the trend toward the more rhythmic type of hymn melody. Triple meter is freely used. In some instances two versions are used, similar to Hoff's procedure, while a number of the old chorale melodies, such as *Ein feste Burg,* are set in strict patterns of even-note movement. It appears that Bielefeldt has gained rhythmic variety, not so much by altering the old melodies as by including new melodies originally with a strong rhythmic movement.

The following excerpts illustrate his melodies of freer rhythmic movement:

DET ER SAA YNDIGT AT FÖLGES AD

No. 35

BLOMSTRE SOM EN ROSENGAARD

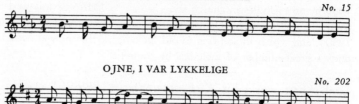

No. 15

OJNE, I VAR LYKKELIGE

No. 202

Other recent publications include the L. Birkedal-Barfod *Menighedens Melodier til Brug i Kirke og Hjem* of 1914.

6

The Chorale in America

IN CHURCHES OF GERMAN BACKGROUND

Immigrants to this country brought their hymnals with them as a matter of course. Since the evangelical church in Germany had not attained a homogeneous hymnody, the early period of the immigrants represents as great a divergence in hymn literature and practice as the localities from which they came in Germany. Thus the Salzburgers who settled in Georgia used the Pietistic Wernigerode hymnbook. In Pennsylvania the Marburg hymnal was widely used. In other places the Coethen Songs and the Württemberg hymn book of 1741 was used. German-Russians used the so-called Volga hymnal, imported from Russia.

German publications in America

The first German hymnal to be published in America was the *Erbauliche Lieder-Sammlung zum Gottesdienstlichen Gebrauch in den Vereinigten Evangelisch-Lutherischen Gemeinden in Nord America*, compiled by a committee instructed by the Ministerium of New York to prepare a hymnal along the order of the Halle hymnbook. It was published in 1786 and contained 706 hymns. The preface was written by Henry Melchior Muhlenberg, patriarch of Lutheranism in America. This publication was replaced by a hymnal prepared by the General Synod in 1843.

In 1849, a new hymnal was published by the Ministerium of Pennsylvania. It was prepared under the editorship of Dr. C. R. Demme, and became popularly known as the Wollenweber book, this being the name of the publisher.

The *Kirchengesangbuch für Evangelisch-Lutherische Gemeinden* compiled and edited by Dr. C. F. W. Walther and his associates became the official hymnal of the Missouri Synod soon after its founding in 1847. The Ohio Synod also published its hymnal in this period.

In a convention of the General Council at Fort Wayne in 1867, a committee was appointed to prepare a new hymnal. This resulted in the *Kirchenbuch,* published in 1877, and extensively used. In 1894, the *Deutsches Gesangbuch* was published for the evangelical Lutheran churches in America by the J. E. Stohlman Company of New York.

The publication of these hymnals and others less widely used, necessitated also the preparation of chorale books to go with them. A chorale book for the first German hymnal, the *Erbauliche Lieder-Sammlung* of 1786, was published in 1813 at the request of the German Evangelical Lutheran Ministerium. This contained 160 musical settings, consisting of melody and figured bass. Since this appears to be the first chorale book published in America, it is a work of unusual interest. The musical settings are rather conservative, quite in line with the practices in Germany at that time. Following is the complete setting of *Vom Himmel hoch,* which may be compared with a setting of the same melody published in Germany in 1817, found on page 85.[148]

---

[148] 46, page 8.

Another important publication of this period was Schmauk's *Deutsche Harmonie*, first published in 1847 and reissued in 1875. This was prepared for *Deutsche Singschulen und Kirchen* and was intended for choir use. Each voice is written on a separate staff, with the melody in the tenor.

The work of Dr. Layriz played an important role in the preparation of German chorale books in America. In 1871, an American edition of the most-used chorales was prepared, taking them from Layriz. It was published in St. Louis under the title *Evangelisch-lutherisches Choralbuch für Kirche und Haus*. The chorales were taken from the second edition of Layriz and given exactly as contained there with the exception of occasionally using a complete bar and a tie instead of setting a half note astride a bar line as is shown in the third example from Layriz on page 108.

In 1879, a chorale book by J. Endlich was published in Philadelphia. It contains also liturgies for the seasons of the church year. The rhythmic patterns of the old chorale melodies are kept quite conservative although there is generous use of triple meter and unusual amounts of irregular rhythm resulting largely from trying to retain old rhythmic patterns in modern notation. Thus, Hassler's melody given as follows:

No. 220

is worse than having no bar lines at all. This is the same version as used in the first edition of Layriz.[149] Hassler's own version of the melody together with its original text is as follows:

Lustgarten, No. 24

Endlich's setting of *Ein feste Burg* is likewise set in modern

---
[149] See page 108.

metrical notation but at the same time tries to retain the older rhythmic pattern.

No. 71

Endlich's chorale book was not based on that of Layriz although the latter appears in a listing of sources consulted by Endlich.

In 1888, a chorale book based on the work of Layriz was published by Karl Brauer in St. Louis. In his foreword to this work, Brauer remarks that:

> Through the second edition of *Kern des deutschen Kirchengesangs* by Dr. Fr. Layriz one congregation after another soon learned to sing the church songs according to the melodies contained therein. One rejoiced in these melodies with their original swinging rhythm. . . .

Brauer's book is essentially a duplicate of the 1871 edition mentioned on page 137. A number of settings are retained exactly; in others new harmonizations have been given in part or almost wholly.

Additional publications representative of this period include the *Liturgie & Choral-Buch* published in Philadelphia in 1897; a *Choralbuch,* published in St. Louis (L. Volkening Verlag) in 1883, and H. J. Holter's *Choralbuch,* used widely in the Missouri Synod.

In 1902, Fr. Lutz published another collection based on the work of Layriz. Selections were made from the different editions. Only minor changes were made, for the most part only bringing the notation up to date, eliminating such practices as setting a half note astride the bar line. His setting of *Ein feste Burg* is in eight-four meter!

English publications in America

The first English hymnbook used in America was a London publication, *Psalmodia Germanica.* Part I was published in 1722 and Part II in 1725. The two parts were combined in a single publication in 1732. It was a translation from the High German. The musical settings consisted of melodies with figured bass.

The first Lutheran hymnbook in English to be published in America was prepared by Dr. J. C. Kunze, assisted by George Strebeck. This undertaking brought forth *A Hymn and Prayer Book, for the use of such Lutheran Churches as use the English Language.* It was published in 1795. About two-thirds of the 239 hymns included in this publication were taken from German sources, many taken either from the *Psalmodia Germanica* or from an English hymnbook for the Moravians published in 1789.

Other English publications were issued by Strebeck in 1797 and by Williston in 1808. The latter was used by the Tennessee, Ohio, and General Synod. In 1814 the Evangelical Lutheran Synod of New York published *A Collection of Hymns and a Liturgy, for the use of Evangelical Lutheran Churches.* Twenty years later *Additional Hymns* was published, which together with the 1814 collection was extensively used.

Rev. Paul Henkel prepared the *Church Hymn Book* in 1816, which was used largely in the Synod of Tennessee, formed in 1820. Several editions of this work appeared—the fourth in 1857.

What appears to have been the most widely used hymnbook of the nineteenth century is *Hymns, Selected and Original, for Public and Private Worship,* published by the General Synod in 1828. The title was somewhat misleading, since two hymns by Dr. S. S. Schmucker, chairman of the hymnal committee, are the only original contributions. The thirty-first edition in 1842 was slightly revised, with an appendix of about 200 hymns added. The book passed through its fifty-sixth edition in 1849. In 1845 the General Synod appointed a committee, headed by Dr. W. M. Reynolds as chairman, to revise the hymnal. The revision was released in 1850, with 759 hymns and an appendix of over 250 hymns. It was used as well in the Joint Synod of Ohio and Other States, formed in 1833, but was replaced by their own publication in 1845, the *Collection of Hymns for Public and Private Worship.* Musical annotations for this work were prepared by Prof. Frederick M. Bird. This hymnal made the transition from the early period of English Lutheran hymnals which contained great numbers of hymns by non-Lutheran writers to a more genuinely Lutheran product, embodying definitely Lutheran traditions and ideals.

The *Evangelical Psalmist,* a collection of tunes and hymns prepared by Drs. Seiss, Mc Cron, and Passavant, was offered to the General Synod as a revised edition of the *Hymns, Selected and Original,* but since the synod did not accept it, the editors published it in 1860 under the above title.

In 1865, *Hymns for the Use of the Evangelical Lutheran Church* was published under the authority of the Ministerium of Pennsylvania. The musical annotations were by Prof. Bird. The hymns in this publication became a part of the *Church Book* published by the General Council in 1868. In 1872, the *Church Book* was issued with music by Harriet Reynolds Krauth and authorized by the General Council. According to the preface, many of the harmonizations were taken from Layriz. Others were taken from the *Chorale Book for England,* published in London in 1865. From "Practical Suggestions" following the preface in this volume, we quote the following:

The importance of frequent meetings for congregational singing, cannot be too strongly urged upon Pastors. An hour in each week, given to the study and practice of church music, will soon enable any congregation to join devoutly and intelligently in every portion of the service.

The fifth edition of the revised *Hymns, Selected and Original,* published in 1852, became the basis of the *Book of Worship,* issued by the General Synod in 1871. A number of new translations from the German were included. There are, however, rather few chorales in this work. There is a marked tendency toward strong rhythmic movement. Running eighth notes in thirds and the dotted eighth-sixteenth figures are frequently met.

The Synod of Missouri, Ohio, and Other States used the *Hymn Book for Use of Evangelical-Lutheran Schools and Congregations,* published in 1879, and the *Hymns of the Evangelical Lutheran Church for the use of English Lutheran Missions,* issued in 1885. The latter contained music.

The Evangelical Lutheran Hymn-Book was published by what was known as the English District of the Evangelical Lutheran Synod of Missouri, Ohio, and Other States, in 1889. In 1905, the *Hymnal for Evangelical Lutheran Missions* was issued, edited by Prof. F. Bente of Concordia Seminary, St. Louis.

In 1880, the *Evangelical Lutheran Hymnal* was issued by order of the Ohio Synod. In 1891, the General Council issued the *Church Book for the Use of Evangelical Lutheran Congregations* in Philadelphia. This was also published by the Wartburg

Publishing House for the Iowa Synod in 1911. This concern issued its own hymnal, the *Wartburg Hymnal,* edited by O. Hardwig, for the Iowa Synod in 1918. The *Book of Worship with Hymns and Tunes* was widely used in the latter part of the nineteenth century and the first quarter of the twentieth.

The Missouri Synod in convention in 1929 authorized a complete revision of its hymnal. This was issued in 1941. In 1918, the merger of thirty-six synods into the present United Lutheran Church in America was completed. The year previous, the *Common Service Book and Hymnal* was published for this church body. The American Lutheran Church, comprising the former Ohio, Iowa, and Buffalo Synods was organized in 1930. Their *American Lutheran Hymnal* was published the same year.

IN CHURCHES OF SWEDISH BACKGROUND

While Swedish colonists had settled on the banks of the Delaware less than a century and a half after Columbus' visit to America, the first permanent growth of Swedish Lutherans came in the nineteenth century in the Middle West. In the days before organs became common in this area, congregational singing was often accompanied by melodeons or psalmodicons. The latter was a string-type instrument on the principle of the guitar. Wallin had been particularly interested in the use of the psalmodicon for church purposes in Sweden, and a special book of melodies for the instrument had been prepared in 1830 by Johann Dillner. It is possible that some of these volumes were used in early Swedish settlements.

Swedish publications in America

Missionaries sent to America took with them copies of the forbidden hymnal prepared by Svedberg. The first Swedish

143

songbook to be printed in America was the first section of *Femtio Andeliga Sänger,* issued in 1856. Its contents were taken largely from the writings of Ahnfelt. "To what extent the book *Femtio Andeliga Sänger* was used at the services in the early period we have no way of determining," writes Evand B. Lawson.[150] "One is inclined to believe that the *Psalmbok* [the official hymnbook of the Church in Sweden] was used in the majority of the pioneer churches," he continues.

In 1860, *Hemlandssånger* was published by the Swedish Lutheran Publication Society. Nearly all of the songs in the previous publication were included and 150 others added. This collection has had a long career. Three thousand copies of the music edition had been printed by 1920 and five thousand copies of the text edition by 1927.

In 1893, the synod adopted as its official hymnal the Thomander-Wieselgren collection which had been issued in Sweden in 1849. An American edition was published in 1886 and again in 1901. Many selections are given two versions, both the Haeffner type and the more rhythmic type.

English publications in America

Meanwhile, a demand for an English hymnal was manifesting itself. The synod, in 1895, instructed the theological faculty at Augustana Seminary to prepare such a hymnal. Four years later a text edition of 355 hymns was submitted and approved. Its musical counterpart, edited by Dr. Alfred Ostrom, was completed in 1901. The liturgy and most of the hymns in this collection were translations from the Swedish. While this hymnal was prepared as a temporary device, it remained in use until 1925 when the present *Hymnal and Order of Service* was authorized.

---

[150] 2, p. 121.

IN CHURCHES OF NORWEGIAN BACKGROUND

Norwegian publications in America

The first Norwegian synod in America was formed in 1846 at Jefferson Prairie, Wisconsin, and called the *Evangelical Lutheran Church in America.* Among the hymnals which the immigrants had with them were Balle's of 1797, Guldberg's of 1778, Kingo's of 1819, and the Harboe-Guldberg hymnal of 1823. Later immigrants brought with them Landstad's of 1869. With them came also Lindeman's *Koralbog.*

The first hymnal to be printed by the Norwegians in America was the Harboe-Guldberg hymnal, printed by Ole Anderson who operated a printing press in Norway, Illinois. This same press put out Pontoppidan's hymnal in 1856. Guldberg's hymnal was printed at Inmansville, Wisconsin, in 1854.

Knud Henderson supplied the first American-published chorale book for the Norwegians in 1865, of which over 25,000 copies were sold. Henderson at this time was only thirty years old. He had very little in common with the Zinck or O. A. Lindeman style which prevailed in his native country in this period. His ideas on rhythmic structure apparently did not meet with universal favor, however, since a copy of the eleventh edition of his book (published in 1900) examined by this writer contains numerous pencil markings in which the rhythmic movement is reduced to notes of more equal durational values.

Olaf Glasöe issued a revision of Ludwig Lindeman's *Koralbog* in 1889 and again in 1899. Only negligible musical changes were made as compared with the original.

English publications

The first English product of the Norwegians was the *Church and Sunday School Hymnal,* issued in 1898. This continued in use until the present *Lutheran Hymnary* was published in 1913.

In 1916, the *Concordia* hymnal was issued, containing both English and Norwegian hymns. In 1933, a completely revised edition, all English, was issued. The most important departure in this work is the large number of Norwegian folk melodies which have been introduced as hymn tunes.

IN CHURCHES OF DANISH BACKGROUND

The first Danish Lutheran church was built at Neenah, Wisconsin, in 1872. The *Salmebog for Kirke og Hjem,* published in Denmark in 1897, has been the accepted hymnal for churches in America using the Danish language. The accompanying chorale book frequently used is *Menighedens Melodier til brug i Kirke og Hjem* by L. Birkedal-Barfod. This contains a total of 1278 musical settings in two volumes, and includes melodies for the above-mentioned hymnal and other commonly used collections.

When the English language came into popular use, the need for an English hymnal was met by using some hymnal already available, particularly the early *Concordia.* The first move toward obtaining their own hymnal in the English language was made by the Danish church bodies in convention in 1924 and 1925. Their hymnal was first published in 1931. A revised and enlarged edition followed in 1938.

7

Present Chorale Problems

THE MELODY

After having followed the development of the chorale as a congregational hymn to this point and having observed this development in the musical illustrations used, there should be no further need to explain why the old chorale melodies are found in so many different versions today. Each church group, accustomed to its own versions of the chorales, has continued to perpetuate these versions. Each group supposes that it has the "correct" versions and wonders why other church bodies sing them differently. It should now be evident that there is no such thing as a correct version.

The one factor which has contributed the most to this diversity of musical settings is the fact that these melodies were written before our present system of musical notation was developed and while musical composition was still in its infancy. Any chorale melody written before the close of the seventeenth century was most likely written in one of the old church modes instead of our modern major and minor scales. As the modern concept of tonality emerged, the old melodies were found awkward in certain melodic progressions and were therefore slightly altered from time to time to fit the new tonality.

Other melodic alterations resulted from fitting a new text to an old melody. So few of our melodies have had a monogamic career. They have been wedded over and over again to texts which in many cases did not fit very well. If one line of verse had one more syllable than the music allowed, a half note was divided into two quarters to make room for the extra syllable. If there were too many notes, it was a simple matter to substitute a longer note for two or more shorter notes or to add the slur sign.

The greatest changes, however, came with the introduction of measured notation in the late seventeenth and eighteenth centuries. The use of the bar line which divided the notation into segments of equal duration determined by a meter signature, played havoc with the notation of the chorale melodies which had come into existence previously.

In this book, twenty illustrations from Luther's *Ein feste Burg* have been given on pages 17, 18, 22, 39, 43, 50, 53, 59, 70, 75, 85, 89, 97, 103, 105, 107, 125, 139. These are, for the most part, *different versions*. There are also ten examples from Luther's *Vom Himmel hoch,* on pages 50, 51, 53, 59, 68, 85, 104, 106, and 137.

An examination of current Lutheran hymnals reveals that no progress has been made in arriving at a single version of the old chorale melodies. Some have continued the practice of omitting bar lines and meter signatures in an attempt to keep the melodies in their original form.[151] Others have crammed the old melodies into modern musical notation resulting in awkward rhythmic movement or a readjustment of note values to make the melodies fit the measure. Some have used mixed

---

[151] Particularly the *Common Service Book and Hymnal,* and the *Evangelical Lutheran Hymn-Book.*

meters, such as changing from four-four to three-four and back again.[152]

Thus to find the "correct" version of an old melody is impossible because there is none. Taking Luther's *Ein feste Burg* as an example, if any version should be given the distinction of being "correct" it should be Luther's own setting. His melody, however, was a product of the plain song technique of his day and cannot be adapted to the modern musical medium without meeting difficulties. Problems exist because while poetical meters were developed long before the time of Luther, the modern concept of musical meters and measures was not achieved until the end of the seventeenth and early eighteenth centuries. The consideration of the relationship of poetical and musical meters is vital because there must be agreement between the accented and unaccented syllables and words of the hymn and the accented and unaccented beats in the musical measure. The general rhythmic flow of the music should agree with that of the text.

The art of music has developed considerably since the sixteenth century. Idioms of musical expression have changed. The composers of the first century of the Reformation used the musical materials available in so far as they had developed at that time. If one were to use the *original* versions of sixteenth century melodies, there would be places where one would be torn between a feeling of natural rhythmic movement and the rhythmic movement the melody calls for.

To illustrate this point, let us consider Hassler's melody to which *O Sacred Head, Now Wounded,* is sung. This was written seventy-five years after the Reformation started and should therefore be considered a rather "modern" melody as compared with the other early chorale melodies.

---

[152] Such as in the *American Lutheran Hymnal,* No. 146.

Hassler wrote the melody without the use of bar lines.[153]
Following are versions of the first phrase of the melody as used
in current hymnals:[154]

Version (a) is sometimes given without meter signature,
sometimes with the signature C which is incorrect in modern
practice. The third phrase of this version is put into a four-four
measure. The opening measure is in six-four, the second is in
three-two (*not* six-four), the third measure is back again in
six-four and the fourth is in three-two. A trained musical organization under a director could follow this but not an unwieldy
group such as a congregation. When a rhythmic pattern is first
established—and this is unconsciously done whether bar lines
are used or not—an inertia is created which will follow through
in repetitions of that basic pattern and cannot easily be persuaded
to change rapidly from one to another.

A congregational hymn tune must, first of all, be simple and
follow a *natural* rhythmic and melodic pattern. The reason why
folk songs on the whole make good hymn melodies is that they
are the simplest and most natural of all music. The imperfection
of our musical notation is only emphasized when a melody
antedating its development is forced into this modern medium

---

153 See page 138.
154 (a) In *The Hymnal* (No. 116), *Lutheran Hymnary* (No. 315), *Common
Service Book and Hymnal* (No. 99), set in four-two meter.
    (b) *Evangelical Lutheran Hymn-Book* (No. 210), *American Lutheran Hymnal*
(No. 383).

of expression. It can seldom be done with a good musical result without altering the melody.

THE UNION OF MUSIC AND POETRY

Another factor which marks a poor hymn is the lack of agreement between text and music. A wholesale rewriting of the texts would be necessary to eliminate all such abuses. As long as we have not only a hymn of four or more stanzas sung to a melody, but often up to a dozen or more hymns to one melody, some of these discrepancies will likely have to exist.

The most serious offences in this phase are of two kinds: where the accented and unaccented syllables or words do not fall on the accented and unaccented beats, respectively, in the music; and where the literary verse does not come to an ending appropriate to the musical cadence. The following illustrations will show the nature of these problems.

Since the first beat in a measure is accented, *by* receives the musical accent, whereas it is plain that *grace* is accented in the poetical construction. A rhythmic setting such as the following, together with reversing the words *I am,* would be more fitting:

The following will illustrate the problem of verse endings failing to agree with musical endings:

In singing this hymn, the first four measures would be one unit because of the very definite cadence on the word *vast*. This would then convey the meaning that God ascended throughout the vast regions of heaven. Obviously, this is not correct. The poetical construction comes to a definite halt after *ascendeth,* but the music does not. To complicate matters further, the music stops on *vast* while the poetical construction is dependent upon the next line to complete the thought.

The classic example of this type of misfit, to be found in almost any hymnal, is the familiar

The musical setting calls for singing "Jesus lives no longer now" since the musical cadence comes at that point.

The reason for these unfortunate misfits is a very basic and simple one. Small musical compositions, such as the hymn, are invariably written in two- or four-measure phrases ending with a more or less complete cadence. This is a way of making music intelligible so that it is not an endless rambling without form. Shorter phrases are balanced against each other to form periods, or sentences, and these in turn make up the complete musical composition. Thus a phrase in music is roughly equivalent to a line of verse. It is perfectly legitimate and often desirable in poetry, however, *not* to come to a halt at the end of each line. Therefore, when the music comes to a natural stop, the poetical expression may be very dependent upon the following line to complete its thought. The degree of disagreement between text and music depends upon the completeness of the musical pause and the incompleteness of the poetical text, or vice versa, at any given point. When a very definite musical stop comes at a poetical point which is wholly dependent upon the following verse, an extremely awkward condition results.

RHYTHMIC VERSUS NONRHYTHMIC CHORALES[155]

Throughout the sixteenth and seventeenth centuries the rhythmic characteristics of the chorale melody in Germany tended to follow the plain song tradition of using notes of equal durational value. When this technique was introduced into Sweden by Haeffner and into Denmark by Thomissön, it met with opposition from the native Scandinavians who preferred their more rhythmic sacred folk song type of hymn melody. Kingo and Pontoppidan carried the matter too far when they introduced dance tunes as hymn melodies. This was the case also with Freylinghausen in Germany.

The even movement of the German chorale provides a very churchly type of melody under certain conditions. It can also become very monotonous and laborious. No one will protest in

---

[155] The term *nonrhythmic* has been used throughout to indicate the style of setting which uses notes of even durational value.

calling *Praise to the Lord, the Almighty* a splendid hymn tune. Yet this moves in even quarter notes in most settings of the melody except for the cadences. In comparing this type of melody with others, one comes to the conclusion that it takes an exceptionally virile melody to overcome the handicap of even-note rhythm. It must have either an objective vigor or a subjective beauty. It must be melodically varied and interesting. The metrical construction of the text can also help or hinder a melody.

The tendency in both the later Scandinavian and German hymnals has been to "restore the original rhythmic movement," meaning the version which existed before the decorative style under Pietism and the extreme even-note style under rationalism. This has been accomplished to some extent.

CONCLUSION

A few general practices have contributed considerably to problems existing in contemporary chorale literature. One of the basic difficulties lies in the fact that there has not been close co-operation between editors of hymnals, who have been pastors, and editors of chorale books or musical versions as found in contemporary hymnals. Hymns have been written for the most part by people who have not understood the intricacies of music. No doubt a writer would have a melody in mind in writing a hymn and would be concerned with achieving an agreement which would be acceptable to his limited understanding of the task of combining the words with the melody. Others may have written hymns with no melody in mind and left it for someone later to find a melody which "fit." This procedure resulted in the rather ridiculous situation of having often up to fifteen and twenty—sometimes over thirty—hymns sung to one melody.

Editors of chorale books do not appear to have been much concerned with hymns. Their interest was in refining the musical medium as the art of music developed from its very crude state. Often alterations were made, both rhythmically and melodically, to suit the particular whims of the day.

In America the situation has not been appreciably improved. Our present music editions of hymnals contain the complete hymn—words and a four-part musical setting. The old faults are still there and are only brought out in bolder relief as a result of this close association of words and music on one page. The relationship of music and text has not been improved to any great extent. One is not convinced that our present hymnals are the product of both competent musicians and competent hymnists.

The Lutheran chorale has had a profound influence upon the development of music as an art and upon church music in particular. The heritage of Lutheran hymnody from its various sources presents today one of the greatest single stores of congregational music and the greatest challenge to the Lutheran church in America to refine and preserve this treasure for posterity.

Appendix

EARLY LUTHERAN SONGBOOKS

A modern reprint of a hymnal prepared by M. Blum and first published in Leipzig in 1530, called the *Enchiridion geistlicher Gesenge und Psalmen,* contains the following list of "the most important oldest Lutheran songbooks":

			Number of hymns
Achtliederbuch		1524	8
Babst	*Gesangbuch*	1545	120
Blum	*Gesangbuch*	1530	63
Breslau	*Breslauer Enchiridion*	1525	38
Herrgott, Hans I	*Nuernberger Enchiridion*	1525	37
Herrgott, Hans II	*Nuernberger Enchiridion*	1527	61
Klug I	*Wittenberger Gesangbuch*	1529	54
Klug II	*Wittenberger Gesangbuch*	1533	54
Klug III	*Wittenberger Gesangbuch*	1535	62
Klug IV	*Wittenberger Gesangbuch*	1543	62
Loerffelt I	*Erfurter Enchiridion*	1525	39
Loerffelt II	*Erfurter Enchiridion*	1525	39
Loerffelt III	*Erfurter Enchiridion*	1526	40
Lufft	*Wittenberger Enchiridion*	1526	42
Maler I	*Erfurter Enchiridion*	1524	26
Maler II	*Erfurter Enchiridion*	1525	38
Maler III	*Erfurter Enchiridion*	1527	63
Schumann	*Schumannsches Gesangbuch*	1539	88
Slüter I	*Plattdeutsch Gesangbuch*	1525	54
Slüter II	*Sluetersches Gesangbuch*	1531	112

Speratus	so-called *Speratusbuch*	1526	(reissue of Slüter I)
Straszburger Enchiridion		1525	26
Sturmer	*Geistliche Gesaenge*	1525	34
Trutebul I	*Erfurter Enchiridion*	1524	26
Trutebul II	*Erfurter Enchiridion*	1524	26
Walther I	*Chorgesangbuechlein*	1524	32
Walther II	*Chorgesangbuechlein*	1525	(2nd edition)
Walther III	*Chorgesangbuechlein*	1537	(3rd edition)
Walther IV	*Chorgesangbuechlein*	1544	(4th edition)
Zwickau I	*Zwickauer Gesangbuch*	1525	26
Zwickau II	*Zwickauer Gesangbuch*	1528	73

It will be noted that five publications came out in 1524, ten in 1525, seven between 1526-1529, and nine between 1530-1545.

HYMNS BY MARTIN LUTHER*

Translations and Arrangements of Latin Hymns	*Hymns based upon Latin Psalms*	
Jesus Christus unser Heiland	Ach Gott vom Himmel	Ps. xii
Verleih uns Frieden gnädiglich	Aus tiefer Noth (2 versions)	Ps. cxxx
Christum wir sollen loben		
Der du bist drei	Ein feste Burg	Ps. xlvi
	Es spricht der Unweisen	Ps. xiv
Herr Gott, dich loben wir		
Komm, Gott, Schöpfer	Es wollt uns Gott	Ps. lxvii
Komm, heiliger Geist	Wär Gott nicht mit uns	Ps. cxxiv
Nun komm der Heiden Heiland	Wohl dem, der in Gottes- fürchte	Ps. cxxviii
Was fürcht'st du Feind		
Wir glauben all' an Einen Gott		

* From Grove's *Dictionary of Music and Musicians.*

Original Hymns
Ein neues Lied
Erhalt uns, Herr'
Jesus Christus, unser Heiland
Nun freut euch
Vom Himmel kam

Amplifications of early German translations of Latin Hymns
Gelobet seyst du
Mitten wir im Leben sind

Corrections or Arrangements of early German Hymns
Christ lag in Todesbanden
Gott der Vater, wohn uns bei
Gott sei gelobet und gebenedeiet
Nun bitten wir den heiligen Geist

Hymns based upon Passages of the Bible

Christ unser Herr	The Baptism of Christ
Diess sind die heiligen zehn Gebot	The Decalogue
Jesaia, dem Propheten	The vision of Isaiah
Mensch, willst du leben	Abbr. version of the Decalogue
Mit Fried und Freud	Nunc Dimittis
Sie ist mir lieb	Rev. xii
Vater unser	Lord's Prayer
Vom Himmel hoch	The Nativity

AN EXPLANATION OF THE FIGURED BASS SYSTEM

Figured bass may be called a system of "musical shorthand" which indicates the complete harmonic structure with only a skeleton outline consisting of the melody and bass. The system came into use with the advent of the harmonic technique at the close of the sixteenth century.

The figures employed indicate the intervals above the bass note, thereby filling in the complete harmonic structure. Hence, 6 indicates that the note six degrees up from the bass note is to be used. This note, together with the soprano and bass already given, will indicate the complete chord. If no figure is given, the bass note is automatically considered to be the root of the chord. Sharps indicate that the third above the bass note is to be sharped.

A solution of *Ein feste Burg* on page 75 follows:

Bibliography

BOOKS

1. Adler, Guido. *Handbuch der Musikgeschichte.* Berlin: Max Hesses Verlag, 1930.
2. *After Seventy-Five Years, 1860-1935. A Jubilee Publication.* Rock Island, Ill.: Augustana Book Concern, 1935.
3. Allard, F. M. *Fra Luther till Bach.* Uppsala: Appelbergs Boktryckeri Actiebolag, 1932.
4. Bachmann, D. Johannes. *Geschichte des evangelischen Kirchengesangs.* Stiller'sche Hof- und Universitäts Buchhandlung, 1881.
5. Beckmann, J. W. *Försök till Svensk Psalmhistoria.* Stockholm: P. A. Norstedt og Sönner, 1888.
6. Benson, Louis F. *The Hymnody of the Christian Church.* New York: Geo. H. Doran Co., 1927.
7. Bergendoff, Conrad. *Olavus Petri and the Ecclesiastical Transformation in Sweden.* New York: The Macmillan Co., 1928.
8. Blume, Friedrich. *Die evangelische Kirchenmusik.* Potsdam: Akademische Verlagsgesellschaft Athenaion M.B.H., 1931.
9. Bobjerg, A. *Den Danske Kirke i Amerika.* Andelsbogtrykkeriet I Odense, 1914.
10. Burney, Charles. *The Present State of Music in Germany.* London: Printed for T. Becket, Strand; J. Robson, New Bond-Street; and G. Robinson, Paternoster-Row, 1775.
11. Finney, Theodore M. *A History of Music.* New York: Harcourt, Brace and Co., 1935.
12. Forsander, Nils. *Life Pictures from Swedish Church History.* Rock Island: Augustana Book Concern, 1913.

_. G. N. S. "Den Svensak Psalmboken," in *Korsbaneret, Kristlig Kalender,* edited by O. N. Olson. Rock Island: Augustana Publishing House, 1919.

14. Hallendorff, Carl and Adolph Schück. *History of Sweden.* London: Cassell & Co., Ltd., 1929.

15. Heydt, Johann Daniel von der. *Geschichte der evangelischen Kirchenmusik.* Berlin: Trowitzsch & Sohn, 1926.

16. Horn, Franz. *Ein feste Burg ist unser Gott, Das Lied der Lieder.* Leipzig: Friedrich Jansa, 1907.

17. Kingo, Thomas. *Aandelige Siunge-koors. Förste part, 4de-udg.* Köbenhavn: Tilkiöbs hos Friderich Jacobsen Brun, 1684.

18. Lambert, J. F. *Luther's Hymns.* Philadelphia: General Council Publication House, 1917.

19. Lang, Paul Henry. *Music in Western Civilization.* New York: W. W. Norton & Co., 1941.

20. Laub, Thomas. *Musik og Kirke.* Kjöbenhavn: Gyldendalske Boghandel, Nordisk Forlag, 1920.

21. Lundblad, G. T. *Förhandlingarne vid Sällskapet "Kyrkosångens Vänners."* Skara: Pettersonska Boktryckeriet, 1899.

22. Lönnquist, C. A. "Den Svenska Psalmboken," in *Korsbaneret, Kristlig Kalender,* edited by C. A. Lindvall. Rock Island: Augustana Publishing House, 1926.

23. Mankell, Abraham. *Musikens Historia.* Clarenden Press, Oxford, 1902.

24. Moberg, Carl Allen. *Kyrkomusikens Historia.* Stockholm: Svenska Kyrkans Diakonistyrelses Bokförlag, 1932.

25. Moser, Hans Joachim. *Die Melodien der Lutherlieder.* Leipzig und Hamburg: Gustav Schloessmanns Verlagsbuchhandlung, 1935.

26. Moser, Hans Joachim. *Geschichte der deutschen Musik. 2 vols.* Stuttgart und Berlin: J. G. Cotta'sche Buchhandlung Nachfolger, 1920.

27. Nelle, Wilhelm. *Geschichte des deutschen evangelischen Kirchenliedes.* Leipzig und Hamburg: Gustav Schloessmanns Verlagsbuchhandlung, 1928.

28. Nodermann, P. *Studier i Svensk hymnologi.* Lund: Sydsvenska bok och musik forlaget, 1911.

29. Nordlie, O. M. *History of the Norwegian People in America.* Minneapolis: Augsburg Publishing House, 1925.

30. Norlind, Tobias. *Svensk Musikhistoria.* Stockholm: Wahlström & Widstrand, 1918.

31. Pick, Bernard. *Luther as a Hymnist.* Philadelphia: Lutheran Book Store, 1875.

32. Polack W. G. *The Handbook to the Lutheran Hymnal.* St. Louis: Concordia Publishing House, 1942.

33. Ryden, Ernest Edwin. *The Story of Our Hymns.* Rock Island: The Augustana Book Concern, 1930.

34. Sandvik, O. M. *Norsk Koralhistorie.* Oslo: H. Aschehoug & Co., 1930.

35. Schauer, Johann Karl. *Dr. M. Luthers Reformationslied "Ein feste Burg ist unser Gott."* Coburg: J. G. Riemann, 1853.

36. Stahl, Wilhelm. *Geschichtliche Entwicklung der evangelischen Kirchenmusik.* Berlin: Max Hesses Verlag, 1920.

37. Stephenson, Geo. M. *The Religious Aspects of Swedish Immigration.* Minneapolis: University of Minnesota Press, 1932.

38. Wilson, Archibald Wayet. *The Chorales; Their Origin and Influence.* London: The Faith Press, Ltd., 1920.

MUSICAL PUBLICATIONS

39. *American Lutheran Hymnal.* Columbus: Lutheran Book Concern, 1930.

40. Bielefeldt, V. *Melodier til Psalmebog for Kirke og Hjem.* 2nd ed. Kjöbenhavn & Leipzig: Wilhelm Hansen Musik-Forlag, 1943.

41. Blum, M. *Enchiridion geistlicher Gesenge und Psalmen.* Leipzig: Reproduced by Barenreiter-Verlag, 1929.

42. Boettner, Johann Christoph. *Choralbuch.* Revised by Heinrich Wegener. Hannover: bei den Gebruldern Hahn, 1817.

43. *Book of Worship With Hymns and Tunes.* Philadelphia: The United Lutheran Publication House, 1899.

44. Brauer, Karl. *Mehrstimmiges Choralbuch.* St. Louis: Concordia Publishing House, 1906.

45. *Choralbuch für die evangelische Kirche in Württemberg.* 3rd ed. Stuttgart: Verlag der J. B. Metzler'schen Buchhandlung, 1876.

46. *Choral-Buch für die Erbauliche Lieder-Sammlung der Deutschen Evangelisch-Lutherischen Gemeinden in Nord-Amerika.* Philadelphia: Conrad Zentler und Georg Blake, 1813.

47. *Church and Sunday School Hymnal.* Minneapolis: Augsburg Publishing House, 1898.

48. *Common Service Book and Hymnal.* Philadelphia: United Lutheran Board of Publication, 1917.

49. *Concordia.* Minneapolis: Augsburg Publishing House, 1933.

50. Crüger, Johann. *Choral-Melodien, aus den besten Quellen streng nach dem Original mitgetheilt von C. E. G. Langbecker.* Berlin: Verlag von G. Eichler, 1835.

51. *Den Swenska Psalmboken af Konungen Gillad och Stadfaestad, år 1819, med Choral-Noter.* Oerebro: N. M. Lindh, 1823.

52. *Deutsches Liederbuch.* Ithaca: Thrift Press, 1934-37.

53. *Dressdenisch Gesangbuch.* Dresden: Churfuerstl. Sachsz Hofe Buchdruckere, 1656.

54. *Das aelteste Zwickauer Gesangbuch von 1525* [Reprint]. Zwickau (Sachsen): Verlag von Johannes Herrmann, 1935.

55. Doles, Johann Friedrich. *Melodien zu des Herrn Prof. C. F. Gellerts Geistlichen Oden und Liedern.* Leipzig: Johann Gottlob Immanual Breitkopf, 1758.

56. Dorsch, Paul. *Das deutsche evangelische Kirchenlied.* Stuttgart: Vereinsbuchhandlung, 1890.

57. Dretzeln, Cornelio Heinrich. *Evangelisches Choral Buch.* Nuernberg: Wolfgang Moritz Endters seel. Tochter, Mayrin und Sohn, 1731.

58. Eccard, Johannes. *Geistliche Lieder nach den Königsberger Original-Ausgaben, 1597.* Edited by G. W. Teschner. Leipzig: Breitkopf & Härtel, ca. 1898.

59. Endlich, J. *Choralbuch mit Liturgie und Chorgesängen.* Philadelphia: The United Lutheran Publication House, 1879.

60. Erhardi, M. Laurentio. *Harmonisches Chor- und Figural Gesang-Buch.* Franckfurt am Mäyn: M. Kempffer, 1659.

61. *Erstes Gesangbuchlein.* Selinsgrove, Pa.: S. E. Ochlenford, 1898.

62. *Evangelical Lutheran Hymn-Book.* St. Louis: Concordia Publishing House, 1930.

63. *Evangelical Lutheran Hymnal.* Columbus: Lutheran Book Concern, 1908.

64. *Evangelisch-Lutherisches Choralbuch für Kirche und Haus.* St. Louis: Verlag von L. Volkening, 1871.

65. Frantz, Klamer Wilhelm. *Choralbuch.* Halberstadt: im Bureau für Literatur und Kunst, 1811.

66. Freylinghausen, Johann Anastasius. *Geistreiches Gesang-Buch.* Halle: Verlegung des Wäysenhauses, 1741.

67. Glasöe, Oluf. *Lindeman's Koralbuch med Tillæg.* Minneapolis: Augsburg Publishing House, 1899.

68. Haeffner, Joh. Christ. Fred. *Svensk Choralbok.* Stockholm: C. Müeller, 1820.

69. Hassler, Hans Leo. *Kirchengesäng, 1608.* Augsburg: Verlegt im Baerenreiter-Verlag, 1927.

70. Hassler, Hans Leo. *Lustgarten.* Edited by F. Zelle. Leipzig: Breitkopf & Härtel, 1887.

71. Henderson, Knud. *Koralbog.* 7th ed. Chicago: John Anderson Publishing Co., 1900.

72. *Hemat, Psalmer och Sanger.* Lindsborg: Bethany Book Concern, 1888.

73. Hentschel, E. *Evangelisches Choralbuch.* 4th ed. Leipzig: Carl Merseburger, 1860.

74. Hillner, Becker, *et. al. Vollständiges vierstimmiges Taschen-Choralbuch mit einfachen Zwischenspielen.* 5th ed. Leipzig: Wilhelm Baensch Verlagshandlung, 1870.

75. Hoff, Eric. *Melodibog.* Kristiania: P. T. Mallings Boghandel, 1876.

76. *Hymnal, The.* Rock Island: Augustana Book Concern, 1925.

77. *Hymnal for Church and Home.* Blair: Danish Lutheran Publishing House, 1938, 1942.

78. Jesperson, Nils. *Gradual,* edited by the Danish Organist and Cantor Association of 1905: København: J. H. Schultz Forlag, 1935.

79. Kalhauge, Viggo. *Fuldstændig Samling af Melodier til Grundtvig's Kirke-Salmebog.* Kjöbenhavn: P. Hemmingsens Tryk, 1876.

80. Kuehnau, Johann Christoph. *Vierstemmige alte und neue Choralgesange.* Berlin: Im Verlag des autors, 1786.

81. Kingo, Thomas. *Gradual, En ny almindelig Kirke-Salmebog.* Trykt i Hans. Kongl. Majestæts privilegerede Trykkerie af Christian Skröder, 1699.

82. Kulke, Martin. *Choralbuch.* Berlin: Verlag der Deutschen Evangelischen Buch- und Traktat-Gesellschaft, 1911.

83. *Kyriale, or Ordinary of Mass.* Baltimore: John Murphy & Co., 1867.

84. Layriz, Dr. Fridrich. *Kern des deutschen Kirchengesangs.* Nördlingen: C. H. Beck 'schen Buchhandlung, 1st ed. 1844, 2nd ed. 1849, 3rd ed. 1853-1855.

85. Lindeman, Ludwig. *Koralbog*. Christiania: J. W. Cappelens Forlag, 1878.

86. Lindeman, Ludwig. *Koralbog med Tillæg*. Minneapolis: Augsburg Publishing House, 1899.

87. Lindeman, O. A. *Choral-Bog, for Kingos, Guldbergs og evangeliskchristelige Psalmebog*. Christiania: Chr. Grøndahl, 1838.

88. Lindström, Albert. *Svenska Psalmboken*. Stockholm: Fröleen & Co., 1892.

89. Lundblad, G. T. *Svensk Koralbok i reviderad rythmisk form*. 2nd ed. Lund: C. W. K. Gleerups Förlag, 1910.

90. *Lutheran Hymnary, The*. Minneapolis: Augsburg Publishing House, 1912.

91. *Lutheran Hymnal, The*. St. Louis: Concordia Publishing House, 1941.

92. Lutz, Fr. *Choralbuch*. Chicago: Wartburg Publishing House, 1902.

93. Lutze, Johann Jakob. *Choralbuch, enthaltend einhundert in Ost- und Westpreuszen gangbare Melodieen*. Koenigsberg: Druck und Verlag der Hartungschen Hofbuchdrukkerei, 1826.

94. *Lose Blätter der Musikantengilde*. Berlin: Georg Kallmeyer Verlag.

95. Mankell, Abraham. *Svensk Psalmboken förenad med dess Koraler*. Stockholm: P. A. Norstedt & Söner, 1865.

96. McHose, Allen I. *Contrapuntal Harmonic Technique of the Eighteenth Century*. New York: F. S. Crofts & Co., 1947.

97. *335 Melodie Deutscher Kirchengesänge after Dr. Fr. Layriz*. St. Louis: Verlag von Volkening, 1887.

98. Mueller, Johann Michael. *Neu-Aufgesetztes Psalm- und Choral-Buch*. Franckfurt am Maeyn: Johann Adolph Stock, 1718-19.

99. Nordqvist, Conrad and Aug. Lagergren. *Svensk Koralbok efter Haeffner*. Stockholm: P. A. Norstedt & Söners Förlag, 1903.

100. Olsson, Otto. *Koralbok för Schola och Hem*. Stockholm: Svenska Kyrkans Diakonistyrelses Bokförlag, 1923.

101. Praetorius, Michael. *Musæ Soniæ*. Edited by Friedrich Blume. Wolfenbüttel-Berlin: Georg Kallmeyer Verlag, 1932.

102. Schmauk, John G. *Deutsche Harmonie, oder Mehrstimmige Gesaenge für Deutsche Singeschulen und Kirchen*. 2nd ed. Philadelphia: Schäfer und Koradi, 1847.

103. Schmidt, Balthasar, *Nürnbergische alte und neue Kirchen-Lieder*. 2nd ed. Nürnberg: J. M. Schmidt, 1773.

104. Speisz, Johann Martin. *Davids Harpffen-Spiel.* Heydelberg: in Verlag Johann Jacob Häners, 1745.
105. Telemann, Georg Philip. *Lieder-Buch.* Hamburg: Gedruckt bey P. L. Stromer, 1730.
106. Terry, Charles S. *J. S. Bach's Original Hymn-Tunes for Congregational Use.* Oxford University Press, 1922.
107. Thomander-Wieselgren. *Koral-Bok med den fulständiga Svenska Messan.* Chicago: The Engberg-Holmberg Publishing Co., 1901.
108. Thomander-Wieselgren. *Svenska Psalm-Boken af år 1819.* Rock Island: Augustana Book Concern, 1892.
109. *Vollstaendige Sammlung theils ganz neu componirter . . . für das neue Wirtembergische Landgesangbuch.* Stuttgart: im Gebrueder Maentler'schen Verlage, 1799.
110. Vulpius, Melchior. *Ein schoen Geistlich Gesangbuch.* Jena (?): 1609 (?).

DICTIONARIES AND CYCLOPEDIAS

111. Davison, Archibald and Willi Apell. *Historical Anthology of Music.* Cambridge: Harvard University Press, 1946.
112. Fuerbringer, L., *et. al. The Concordia Cyclopedia.* St. Louis: Concordia Publishing House, 1927.
113. *Grove's Dictionary of Music and Musicians.* 5 Vols. London: Macmillan & Co., 1928.
114. Jacobs, Henry E., and John A. S. Haas. *The Lutheran Cyclopedia.* New York: Charles Scribners & Sons, 1899.
115. Julian, John. *A Dictionary of Hymnology.* London: John Murray, 1907.
116. Koch, Eduard Emil. *Geschichte des Kirchenlieds und Kirchengesangs.* Stuttgart: Chr. Belser'schen Verlagshandlung, 1867.
117. Kümmerle, S. *Encyklopädie der Evangelischen Kirchenmusik* (4 volumes). Gütersloh: Bertelsmann, 1888-95.
118. Schweitzer, Albert. *J. S. Bach.* London: A & C. Black, Limited, 1938.
119. Spitta, Johann August. *Johann Sebastian Bach.* London: Novello & Co., 1899.
120. Thuner, O. E. *Dansk Salme-Leksikon,* Köbenhavn: O. Lohse, 1930.
121. *Works of Martin Luther.* Philadelphia: A. J. Holman Co.
122. Zahn, Johannes. *Die Melodien der Deutschen Evangelischen Kirchenlieder.* 6 Vols. Gütersloh: Bertelsmann, 1889-93.

Index

Type used in this book

Body, 12 on 14 and 10 on 11 Garamond

Display, Garamond bold